ULTIMATE SUDOKU
FUN BOOK
IT'S A BLAST!

508
SUDOKU PUZZLES

creative EDGE

If you can count to nine, you can play **SuDoku!** Seriously.

You don't have to be good at math, you don't have to have a super memory, and you don't even need a big vocabulary. You just need to figure out where the numbers go.

But we'll get to that in a minute. Let's start at the very beginning. Sudoku is a Japanese word—an abbreviation of a phrase meaning "the digits must remain single." In other words, you can't have two of the same number in the same line or box. Some people call it SOO-doe-koo, and others say soo-DOE-koo. We just call it plain 'ol fun.

Interestingly enough, even though the game has a Japanese name, the Japanese didn't invent it. Sudoku appeared as "Number Place" in an American game magazine in 1979, but the Japanese refined it and renamed it after that.

Sudoku is played on a grid, and it usually includes nine small squares inside nine larger boxes. Each line going across is called a row, and each line going up and down, a column. **(See Figure A)**

When you first look at a Sudoku grid, you'll notice something interesting. Some of the numbers have already been filled in. How many numbers there are and where they're placed has a lot to do with how hard the puzzle will be to solve. But don't worry. We'll start off easy.

Now, as we mentioned earlier, you can't have two of the same number in a line or box. Your goal, then, is to fill in the squares one at a time so that each column includes the numbers one through nine, each row includes the numbers one through nine, and each box includes the numbers one through nine. Figure B is a completed Sudoku grid. Notice how the numbers don't repeat? **(See Figure B)**

Figure A

column · *row* · *box*

8								4
	2		1	9		7		
		9	5				2	
3	9		8			4	6	
4		2		6		5		8
	6	8			2		1	7
	7		9			6	2	
		6		8	1		7	
9							4	

Figure B

7	8	5	6	2	3	1	9	4
6	2	3	1	9	4	7	8	5
1	4	9	5	7	8	6	2	3
3	9	7	8	1	5	4	6	2
4	1	2	7	6	9	5	3	8
5	6	8	3	4	2	9	1	7
8	7	4	9	3	6	2	5	1
2	5	6	4	8	1	3	7	9
9	3	1	2	5	7	8	4	6

Now you've got an idea of what the puzzle is supposed to look like when you're through. Ready to learn how to get there? Consider trying the first one with a family member or friend! It's not that we don't think you're smart enough to figure it out on your own. Different people see things in different ways, and you'll be able to help each other out. One person, for example, might focus on the numbers in the columns or rows first; another might focus on the numbers in the box; and someone else might use different logic altogether to decide which number goes where. All three ways are helpful, and if someone sees something you don't, ask them to explain. The more ways you can learn to solve a puzzle, the better you'll become at solving problems in real life, too.

Now, let's give it a shot. Let's say your Sudoku grid contains the numbers 3, 5, 7, 2, 1, 8, 6 and 9 across the top row. It might look something like this: **(See Figure C)**

Know which number is missing?

That's right; it's the 4. So you can already fill one space in. Celebrate your victory, then get ready to move on.

Let's say the grid has a box that looks like this: **(See Figure D)**

Which number is missing now?

Right again! It's the 5 that's missing.

Figure C

3	5		7	2	1	8	6	9

Figure D

			9	6	7			
				2	8			
			4	1	3			

But what happens when more than one number is missing in a row, column, or box? You'll have to reason it out. Take this grid, for example. Can you figure out where the next 6 will go? **(See Figure E)**

Sure you can! Since each row can only have one 6, and each box can only have one 6, you can reason that the next 6 will go on the bottom row of the far right box, next to the 4. Getting the hang of it?

When you start a Sudoku puzzle, then, look for places where you have two of a kind, or two out of three boxes next to each other containing the same number. At the same time, look for places where a certain number is missing in your one-to-nine lineup in a box, row, or column. Let's take a look at how you can use those techniques together.

Maybe you've moved ahead on the last grid so it looks like this: **(See Figure F)**

First of all, take a look at the second box down on the right. Count it out, and you'll see that the blank space should be a 3, right? Every other number is already represented in the box. That new 3, however, affects more than you think it does. You can use that 3 to figure out where the 3 will go in the box above it, as well. Look closely at the second and third rows. See how they already have 3s, but the first row doesn't? Remember that you can't have the same number twice in the same row, so the 3 of the top right box has to go in the top row. With us so far? It looks like that 3 could go in either of the two empty squares in the top right box. But remember that 3 we just placed? Again, you can't have two of the same number in any column. So it can't go in the same line as the new one. It has to go in the far right square.

Figure E

Figure F

While you're trying to figure out a Sudoku puzzle, you may come to a square that looks as if it could hold one of two numbers. If that's the case, it's OK to lightly pencil-in both numbers in a corner of the square, until you get another clue that helps you know for sure. Sometimes you have to rule out every number a square is *not* before you know what number it actually is. Remember that no matter how hard the puzzle seems at first, you've been given everything you need to solve it. There's no need to guess.

You'll find that the puzzles in this book will get more and more challenging as you go along. But you'll probably also notice that you're better and better at solving them.

Sudoku puzzles usually contain nine small squares inside nine larger boxes. The puzzles pictured here, however, begin with grids built on four. Those are called No Brainers. **(See Figure G)**

Easy as Pie and Middle of the Road puzzles, built on grids of six, come next. **(See Figure H)**

The remainder of the puzzles in this book are traditional, nine-grid Sudoku games.

Remember that each puzzle will take some thought, some patience, and some logic. All that—and, simply, the ability to count from one to nine.

Have fun!

Figure G

Figure H

Puzzle 1

			1
	1		4
1		4	
2			

Puzzle 2

	2		
1		3	
	3		1
		2	

Answers on Page 262

2	3	4	1
4	1	2	3

	3		1
	1		
		2	
3		1	

Puzzle 5

1			
		4	1
4	3		
			4

Puzzle 6

3	4		
2	1		
		1	2
		3	4

Answers on Page 262

Puzzle 7

3			
			4
4			
			2

Puzzle 8

4			2
2			3
1			4
3			1

Answers on Page 262

Puzzle 9

	3		
		2	
	1		
		3	

Puzzle 10

	2	3	
	4	2	
	3	1	
	1	4	

	4	1	2
2	3	4	

			2
	4	3	
	2	1	
3			

Puzzle 13

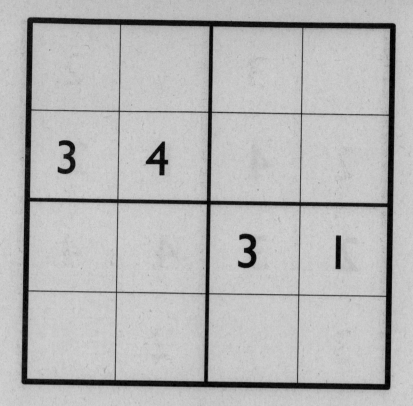

Puzzle 14

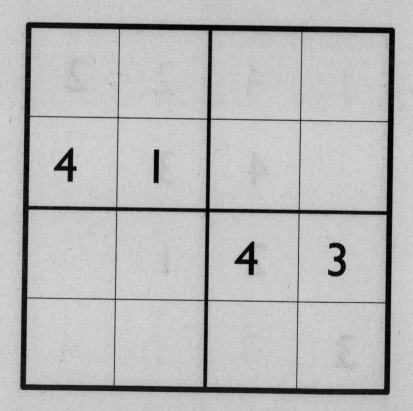

Answers on Page 263

	3		2
2			
			4
3		2	

1	4	2	3
2	3	1	4

Puzzle 17

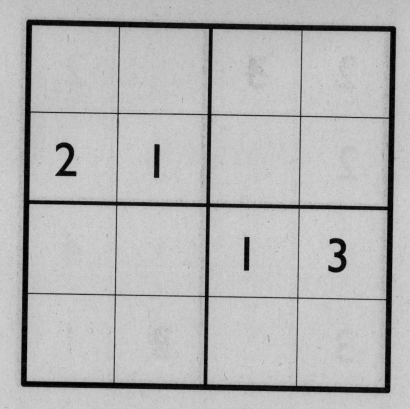

Puzzle 18

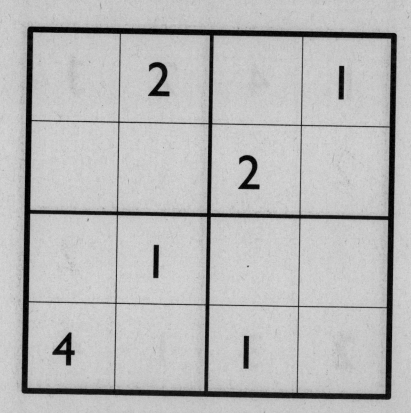

Answers on Page 263

Puzzle 19

2	4		
		4	1

Puzzle 20

			1
2			
			2
3			

Puzzle 21

	1		4
		1	
	2		
1		4	

Puzzle 22

4		1	
1			
			2
	4		1

Answers on Page 263

Puzzle 23

3	1		
		3	4

Puzzle 24

		1	2
4	1		

Answers on Page 263

Puzzle 25

2			4
		3	
	4		
3			1

Puzzle 26

3			4
	1		
		3	
2			1

Answers on Page 264

Puzzle 27

3	1		
		2	3

Puzzle 28

		3	2
4	2		

Puzzle 29

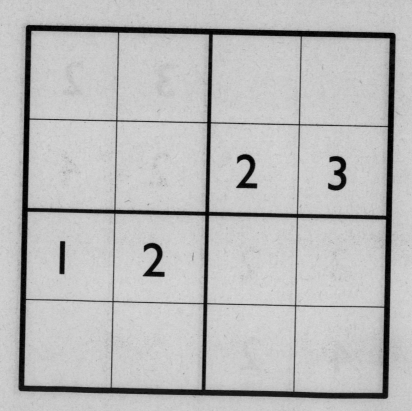

Puzzle 30

Answers on Page 264

		3	4
3	1		

		2	4
3	2		

Puzzle 33

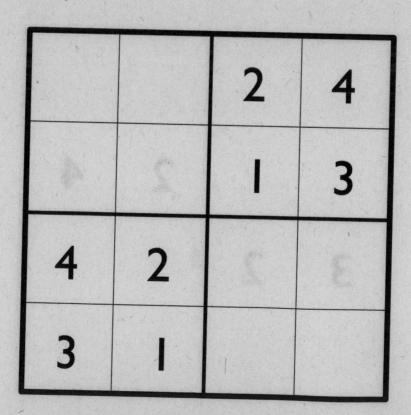

Puzzle 34

Answers on Page 264

2			
			1
4			
			2

1			
	2		1
4		2	
			4

Answers on Page 265

Puzzle 37

1	4	2	3
4	2	3	1

Puzzle 38

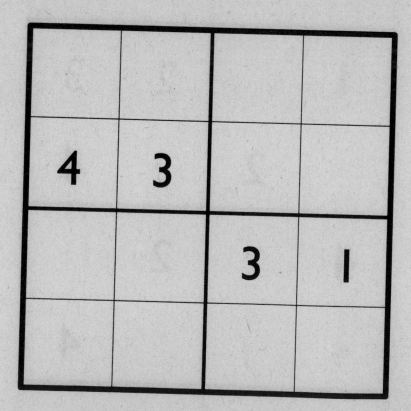

4	3		
		3	1

Answers on Page 265

Puzzle 39

2		4	
			3
3			
	2		4

Puzzle 40

		2	3
		1	4
3	2		
4	1		

Answers on Page 265

Puzzle 41

			2
	3		1
1		2	
3			

Puzzle 42

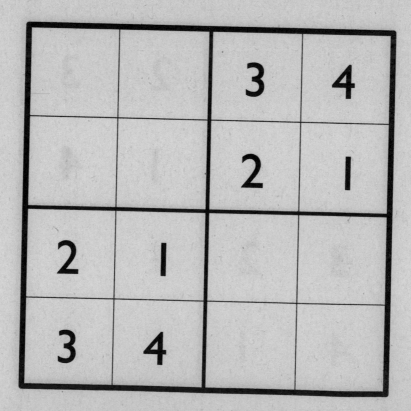

		3	4
		2	1
2	1		
3	4		

Answers on Page 265

	4		1
3			
			3
1		4	

1			
	4		1
4		1	
			2

Puzzle 45

			6	3	
		6			5
6				4	
	2				6
1			5		
	5	2			

Puzzle 46

3				5	
	6	4	1		
					5
1					
		3	5	2	
	1				6

Answers on Page 265

Puzzle 47

				1	5
	4	5			
		2	5		4
6		4	2		
			1	4	
4	3				

Puzzle 48

5				1	6
		1	4		
		3			
			1		
		4	5		
3	2				1

Puzzle 49

	1		3	2	
					5
4				3	1
1	3				4
2					
	4	6		1	

Puzzle 50

1		5		3	
	3		6		
	5		1		
		3		5	
		1		6	
	4		3		1

Answers on Page 266

		1			6
4					3
			5		
		2			
1					4
6			2		

		3	5	6	
	5		3		1
2		1		4	
	1	5	4		

Puzzle 53

	1		2		
2	5		6		
	3				
				6	
		4		1	2
		1		3	

Puzzle 54

			5		
	1			3	
	6			4	2
4	3			5	
	4			6	
		6			

Answers on Page 266

4	1				
2				1	5
			1		6
5		1			
6	2				1
				2	3

4		6			
1	2	5			
	4				6
6				2	
			1	6	2
			4		5

Puzzle 57

6		4	2		
				3	
	1	6			3
5			4	1	
	6				
		2	3		5

Puzzle 58

			2		
1					6
		3		6	
	6		3		
4					5
		2			

Answers on Page 266

			3		
			6	1	4
			2	3	6
6	3	2			
3	1	4			
		5			

	2		3	4	
				2	1
			4		
		4			
3	6				
	1	2		5	

Puzzle 61

1	6				
	3	5	1		
6					
					2
		2	6	1	
				3	5

Puzzle 62

4	2			6	
5					4
2				3	
	3				5
1					3
	5			1	2

Answers on Page 267

4		1	6		
		2		4	
			3		
		3			
	3		4		
		6	1		3

				6	3
4				2	
6			3	1	
	1	4			6
	4				2
1	3				

Puzzle 65

	4		1		
			2		
	3	6		2	
	1		6	3	
		3			
		1		6	

Puzzle 66

	6	4			5
	3	1		4	
	5		1	3	
3			6	5	

Puzzle 67

	4			2	
1					5
		2		1	6
6	1		2		
2					3
	5			4	

Puzzle 68

	2				
1			5		3
4			6		
		2			4
6		4			5
				6	

Puzzle 69

6		1		4	
			2		6
	1	3			
			3	5	
4		6			
	5		6		4

Puzzle 70

	1		6		
3	6		2		
				2	6
1	2				
		1		5	2
		4		6	

Answers on Page 267

Puzzle 71

			1		
5	3				
			3	5	6
6	5	3			
				6	2
		5			

Puzzle 72

4			1		
3			2	4	
	6		5		
		5		6	
	3	4			2
		1			3

Puzzle 73

2			3		
				2	5
	3	4			
			1	3	
5	4				
		1			6

Puzzle 74

		5	1		2
	1	6		4	5
5	4		6	2	
3		1	5		

Answers on Page 268

Puzzle 75

6	5				
			5	1	
	1			5	3
2	3			6	
	2	3			
				2	5

Puzzle 76

			6	2	4
6			5		
	1				
				4	
		6			3
1	3	4			

Puzzle 77

6		5			
	3	4			
			2	4	
	4	6			
			3	1	
			5		2

Puzzle 78

			5	6	
1		6			4
		5		4	
	4		2		
3			4		6
	6	4			

Answers on Page 268

4					3
			5	4	
	4				1
6				3	
	1	6			
2					5

	2	1	4	5	
		6			1
2			5		
	5	4	2	3	

Puzzle 81

6			2	5	
			3		
			1		5
5		1			
		2			
	5	3			6

Puzzle 82

					5
			4	6	
5		6	2		
		2	6		1
	6	4			
1					

Answers on Page 268

	5				
	1			6	4
4			3		
		3			6
2	4			5	
				4	

6		4			3
5	3				
				2	
	5				
				1	5
1			2		6

Puzzle 85

	1				5
		3			
					1
5					
			6		
4				3	

Puzzle 86

		1			6
				4	
			2		
		3			
	6				
2			3		

Answers on Page 269

				2	
	5				
2			3		
		3			5
				6	
	4				

5			4		
	1				
			1		
		3			
				3	
		6			5

Puzzle 89

			4		
			2	1	
					3
1					
	5	3			
		4			

Puzzle 90

5				1	
		4			
				3	
	6				
			5		
	3				6

Answers on Page 269

			1		
	6				2
				4	
	3				
4				3	
		2			

		2			5
	4				
6					
					1
				2	
1			6		

Puzzle 93

			2	3	
				4	
2					
					5
	4				
	1	5			

Puzzle 94

	4		1		
			3		
				2	
	6				
		5			
		2		6	

Answers on Page 269

3					
4	5				
		6			
			5		
				2	6
					3

		4			3
			1		
					5
1					
		5			
6			4		

Puzzle 97

	3				
	1				
6					5
5					3
				4	
				6	

Puzzle 98

		3			
		2		5	
	1				
				4	
	4		1		
			6		

Answers on Page 270

Puzzle 99

	2				
4			5		
			3		
		6			
		3			6
				4	

Puzzle 100

5			3		
				6	
					5
3					
	1				
		6			4

Puzzle 101

	5		1		
	3				
			5		
		4			
				4	
		6		3	

Puzzle 102

				6	
				5	
		5	2		
		2	3		
	3				
	1				

Answers on Page 270

	2				
	3				
4					5
5					3
				4	
				6	

1				2	
4					
	3				
				1	
					3
	5				4

Puzzle 105

	5				1
		2			
					5
1					
			4		
6				2	

Puzzle 106

					2
					3
	2			6	
	6			5	
1					
5					

Answers on Page 270

Puzzle 107

					5
					6
		2	1		
		5	2		
1					
4					

Puzzle 108

6				1	
4					
	3				
				5	
					2
	5				3

Puzzle 109

				3	
		2		5	
		5			
			2		
	6		1		
	4				

Puzzle 110

6				1	
				2	
					5
4					
	3				
	5				4

Answers on Page 271

		6			
	2				1
					2
1					
3				6	
			5		

		6			4
					3
			6		
		4			
2					
5			1		

Puzzle 113

	5				
	2				
3					5
4					3
				1	
				4	

Puzzle 114

				5	
		4		2	
		2			
			1		
	5		3		
	1				

Answers on Page 271

Puzzle 115

	6				
	2				3
4					
					5
5				4	
				1	

Puzzle 116

		1			
	5				6
2					
					1
3				5	
			2		

Puzzle 117

				1	
		3		6	
			3		
		6			
	2		4		
	5				

Puzzle 118

		2			
	4		3		
				2	
	5				
		3		1	
			5		

Answers on Page 271

Puzzle 119

	1				
2				5	
					1
3					
	5				6
				3	

Puzzle 120

		1		5	
					4
		4			
			3		
3					
	5		6		

Answers on Page 271

Puzzle 121

		6			
	5				2
4					
					3
3				4	
			5		

Puzzle 122

	1				2
			3		
	6				
				5	
		2			
5				6	

Answers on Page 272

		2			
		3			
1					2
6					1
			5		
			6		

				1	
				6	
6					5
5					3
	4				
	3				

Puzzle 125

	8							4
	2		1	9		7		
		9	5		8		2	
3	9		8			4	6	
4		2		6		5		8
	6	8			2		1	7
	7		9		6	2		
		6		8	1		7	
9							4	

Puzzle 126

1	9			5	4			
5	7	3		2		8	9	
				3		7		
		1		6			2	
		4	2		7	1		
	6			9		3		
		9		4				
	4	2		1		9	8	3
			8	7			4	1

Answers on Page 272

Puzzle 127

	8	5		6			1	9
9	1		3			7		5
	7	2		9			6	
		7	9					8
				5				
1					8	3		
	6			1		9	4	
5		9			2		1	7
2		1		7		5	8	

Puzzle 128

	7		5				6	
	6			8	9			4
8	4	3	6		7			
5			4	7				
		4	1	9	5	6		
				3	6			1
			8		2	5	1	7
2			7	5			4	
	5				4		8	

Answers on Page 272

Puzzle 129

		3			4	2	5	
8	4		5	3	7	1		
1		9	2					4
		7		4				3
3								7
9				2		5		
5					8	7		2
		8	9	5	2		3	1
	9	6	3			4		

Puzzle 130

2		9		5				
		4		7	1	8		9
			9			1		
1		6	2				7	3
	9	5				2	6	
7	3				6	5		1
		7			4			
9		1	5	8		6		
				2		3		5

		1	3					
	9	3	1			5	6	
6	4	7				3	1	
				8	1			4
			6	4	7			
7			2	9				
	7	6				8	3	5
	2	8			3	4	7	
				7		2		

	2	4					5	
		7	4			2		9
		8	3					
7		1	9		8		2	
	4		1			3		8
	5		2		6	1		3
					4	7		
2		6			9	4		
	7					8	9	

Puzzle 133

8				7	9		1	
	6	4			3			
	7		6			8		
		8		1	5		6	
6	9			2			4	3
	5		9	4		2		
		3			2		5	
			8			3	7	
	8		5	3				2

Puzzle 134

8				2				5
	6					1		
2	3	7				9		4
		6			1	3	4	9
		4	6	7	9	8		
9	1	2	8			7		
6		9				5	3	1
		3					9	
1				9				7

Answers on Page 273

	2			8	3	9	1	
			9				3	2
3			2		1	5	6	
	3				8		5	
6			4		9			2
	1		5				7	
	4	2	3		7			6
	5	3			2			
	6	9	8	1			3	

		2		6	1			9
			9			2	4	
	4	9			5	7		8
3	8			1				7
	1		7		9		6	
9				8			5	1
7		3	2			1	8	
	6	1			3			
4			1	5		6		

Puzzle 137

		2		8	1			9
		6	4	2	5			
3								1
8						3	5	
5	3	4				8	9	7
	9	7						4
4								3
			7	6	3	4		
2			8	9		6		

Puzzle 138

6		3	7					8
		8		4	3	5	2	
	7				9			3
				3				2
7	3	1		2		8	9	5
8				7				
5			3				7	
	9	6	2	8		4		
1					4	3		9

Answers on Page 273

	6	7	8	1	5		3	
8		9			3		6	
1								
		1		5	2	4		3
	7						1	
3		4	1	6		8		
								4
	4		6			5		7
	5		3	2	4	6	9	

		6	1		5		3	9
9		7				5		
2	3							
7	9	4		5	2	1	6	
			3		7			
	2	3	9	6		8	7	4
							8	6
		9				4		5
4	6		5		3	2		

Puzzle 141

	7		4					9
	4	1	9	6				5
		6			5	2		
	8			7	6	4		
	6		3	8	1		5	
		5	2	4			8	
		3	8			7		
9				3	4	8	1	
8					7		3	

Puzzle 142

	1	2	8	3				
9		5		2	7	6		
4		3		1	6			
			2			5		7
8			6		3			1
7		4			1			
			3	8		1		9
		1	7	9		4		5
				6	4	3	7	

Answers on Page 273

			8		5			1
3				6			2	5
						7	8	3
7	1	4	2	8		5		6
			4		9			
5		2		7	6	4	3	8
1	2	5						
6	3			9				4
9			6		1			

					1			8
	1	8		5		4	3	9
			4	6		7		
1		6	5		2			
7		5				1		2
			6		3	8		7
		3	1	2				
8	6	1		3		2	9	
4			9					

Puzzle 145

	3		7	9	1	4		
			2					7
7		4	6			2	1	
		9			8	6	2	5
4								1
6	5	8	1			7		
	6	1			7	8		4
8					2			
		7	8	6	5		9	

Puzzle 146

7	9	8			2		3	
		2		5				4
	5			9	6		2	
	3		6	7	1		9	
	7						5	
	1		5	8	9		4	
	8		1	2			6	
6				4		5		
	4		7			2	8	1

Answers on Page 274

Puzzle 147

	5	3		7		9	6	8
					1		3	
	2	9			5		7	
8			7			1		6
	7						8	
4		6			8			3
	6		4			3	1	
	1		3					
3	8	2		1		6	9	

Puzzle 148

	7	6	9			4		5
4	2				8			
9			7				6	8
				5		2		
6	8			9			7	4
		2		1				
7	3				5			2
			1				5	3
1		8			9	6	4	

Answers on Page 274

Puzzle 149

3		6	9		5	1	2	
			6	7			5	4
2	5	7		4			9	
						2	4	1
1	6	4						
	8			2		9	1	6
6	9			3	1			
	2	1	7		6	8		5

Puzzle 150

			2	8	3			4
	1					3	9	2
		6	9				5	8
5		1		4	8			
	6	2				8	4	
			1	6		9		5
6	2				1	5		
3	8	7					1	
1			3	2	7			

Answers on Page 274

	7						1	
				1	4	2		6
					6	9	5	
4	9	7			2	1		
2	3	1		7		4	9	5
		6	1			7	2	3
	1	9	8					
8		4	9	5				
	6						3	

	3				5			7
				8	7	3		1
		8		9	2	5		
	9		7			2	5	8
	8	7				4	6	
4	2	6			8		1	
		4	2	1		9		
7		3	4	5				
2			8				3	

Puzzle 153

	2	8		1			7	5
		9			6	4	8	
				5	4			
	4				8		1	9
		6	4	9	1	2		
9	8		2				4	
			1	3				
	1	7	6			9		
3	9			4		8	6	

Puzzle 154

4	7					8	6	
		6		4				1
	3		9		6			
6		7	5			9		
	4	3	6		9	1	2	
		9			7	5		6
			7		4		1	
3				2		6		
	2	1					9	5

Answers on Page 274

9			4		1	8	7	5
					6	9		2
7	4							
			5				1	8
4	2	8		9		5	6	7
3	5				7			
							8	6
1		9	7					
5	3	6	2		8			4

	6			3		1		
				7	2	5	3	
		7		1		2	6	
	2	4	1	5			7	
		9	2		7	3		
	1			6	9	4	5	
	9	5		8		6		
	4	8	5	2				
		6		9			1	

Puzzle 157

	4	2			7			
3						7		8
5	7	6	8	9		2	1	
			3		1	5	2	
	6	5	7		4			
	1	4		3	8	6	9	5
2		9						3
			4			1	7	

Puzzle 158

2					9			1
9		4		6				
			1	3				6
	7	5	6	2		1		
4		6	3		1	2		8
		8		4	7	5	6	
5				8	3			
				1		8		2
6			7					4

Answers on Page 275

Puzzle 159

			4	6				9
9	6	8						3
	4	3	9			1	6	
4			2			6	1	
1				7				5
	8	2			6			4
	1	9			8	4	5	
8						9	2	6
5				9	7			

Puzzle 160

	9		4			3		
			9	5		2	8	6
2		3		8				1
	4		5	1		6	3	
				3				
	3	2		9	6		7	
5				4		7		2
3	2	7		6	9			
		4			5		1	

Puzzle 161

		5	6		8	1	2	
				7		4		
			1	5	4			6
6	8				7	2	3	
		7	5		1	9		
	5	9	2				7	1
3			8	1	9			
		4		3				
	1	6	4		5	3		

Puzzle 162

	1				2	5		
			7	6				4
4	3					7		2
8		4		3	7	1	5	
		5	6		4	2		
	6	3	5	9		8		7
9		6					2	3
7				5	3			
		1	4				7	

Answers on Page 275

Puzzle 163

5	6				8		3	9
		1			2	7		6
2	7	9	4			1	8	
				2		6		
	5						9	
		6		7				
	1	2			5	9	7	3
9		5	2			8		
7	3		1				2	4

Puzzle 164

	1			8		7	3	6
	8	3		6	2		5	9
	4							
			2			3		
	7	4		9		5	6	
		8			7			
							7	
1	9		8	3		6	4	
8	2	5		4			9	

Puzzle 165

7			4	6	1			
	4	9	7					3
	5				9			4
		5		1		2		6
3	9			4			5	1
1		6		7		4		
9			6				1	
5					2	3	4	
			3	9	7			2

Puzzle 166

	1	3					6	
7		6	8				1	5
		8		6	2		7	
3	5			2		7		
	6		8		7		2	
		2		4			9	3
	8		6	9		1		
6	3			1		4		9
	4					2	8	

Answers on Page 275

Puzzle 167

	9					8	4	
				1	6	3		
	7	3			9	2	1	
			5	2			8	
8		9				5		4
	6		4	7				
	3	1	5			7	9	
		4	2	6				
	5	2					6	

Puzzle 168

	3	7		8		6		1
6		8			3	4	2	7
5								
	8			2		1		
	5		1	7	9		3	
		1		6			4	
								3
7	4	3	6			5		8
1		5		3		2	9	

Puzzle 169

	1		7				3	
	7	3		8				
4	9				1	7		
8			9			1	4	7
9	5		4		7		6	8
7	3	4			8			5
		7	6				1	3
				7		8	9	
	4				5		7	

Puzzle 170

		8		5				6
	1		4			7		2
			1		8			
	8	3		1	5			
	2	9	6		3	8	7	
			7	8		3	9	
			3		4			
3		2			1		4	
1				7		5		

Answers on Page 276

				6				7
	7					6	1	5
6		9						
7	5	1	6	2		9	8	
			7	4	8			
	8	2		9	5	7	3	6
						3		1
9	1	3					7	
2				1				

1		4	5		3	7		6
		6			2		3	
5		3	9			1	4	
		2						9
8	6						1	5
7						2		
	5	8			4	9		7
	9		7			4		
3		7	8		9	6		1

Puzzle 173

			7	3			8	
					1	5		3
9			2	6	5		1	
	4		3			8		5
1	2						3	4
3		9			7		2	
	5		4	2	8			9
8		4	9					
	9			5	6			

Puzzle 174

							2	
		1				8	6	3
		2	3	9			1	
		3	4	7		2	5	
5	6		1	3	2		7	8
	2	8		6	9	4		
	8			5	7	3		
2	7	6				1		
	4							

Puzzle 175

				3	2		9	
				6	9	8	3	4
9	8	3	5		1			2
4						6		
8	1						2	9
		5						7
1			9		6	2	5	3
3	9	8	2	1				
	5		4	7				

Puzzle 176

						5	1	
8	4	5			9			
	7		8		2			4
	8		3	7				1
6	5			2			4	3
7				1	6		9	
4			7		5		8	
			6			4	2	9
	6	8						

Puzzle 177

	8	1	6	2	4			
	6					2		
	2	7	9					4
	4	6			1		2	
2			8	6	5			7
	7		2			3	1	
7					6	5	3	
		8					4	
			5	1	2	9	7	

Puzzle 178

		7			3		2	
	9	2		8	5		6	
	3							4
		3	1					
4	8	6	3		7	1	9	5
					8	2		
3							8	
	6		5	1		7	3	
	5		8			4		

Answers on Page 276

	8	9						
1		6		7	8	5		
		4			6		3	9
6	1			2				
	2	3				1	7	
				3			4	2
7	6		1			4		
		5	2	6		3		7
							2	5

		7		5		6		
5					6			2
	8	6		2		9		5
6		3			5			
1	7	5		9		8	3	6
			3			7		4
3		8		1		4	9	
9			6					3
		1		3		2		

Puzzle 181

3						6	7	
	9			8			2	
	6			2	7	8		1
	3	8		5				
4	1			6			9	7
				9		5	4	
7		9	8	3			5	
	5			1			6	
	4	1						3

Puzzle 182

				1	3	6	9	8
			2		9	5	3	
		9	5	4				1
		5					4	6
	1	7				8	5	
2	4					9		
9				5	2	1		
	5	1	8		7			
7	6	2	9	3				

Answers on Page 277

Puzzle 183

	9	1	2			8	6	
5		3	6	1	7	2		
		2					5	
9	6	4	1					
				4				
					5	4	2	6
	4					9		
		9	5	6	8	1		3
	5	8			9	6	7	

Puzzle 184

2			1			8		4
1			6	2			3	5
	5			7		6		
		2	5	4	7		6	
	4		2	9	1	5		
		9		1			4	
7	6			3	4			9
4		3			5			8

Puzzle 185

1	6		3			8		
7						4	1	
3		8	1					5
		1		9	2	6	5	
4				5				7
	7	9	4	3		1		
6					7	5		9
	8	7						6
		4			8		7	1

Puzzle 186

8						9		
				1	9		2	4
		3	4			5	7	
2				9			3	
7	5	1	2		3	6	9	8
	9			6				5
	3	7			8	4		
5	6		1	3				
		9						2

Answers on Page 277

6				1			5	
	2	7		8				9
1		5				4	8	7
		8			9		3	2
		3	8		6	9		
9	4		2			8		
3	6	2				7		1
5				2		3	9	
	9			7				6

	3	1			6	7		
6		5	7		8		2	
8			5					9
	1		4				3	6
	8	6				2	9	
3	2				7		4	
7					2			4
	9		6		4	3		5
		4	9			6	7	

Puzzle 189

	7				8			
2		8	4		9		1	3
6		4	5			7	8	9
	2				6	8		4
3		1	2				5	
5	4	3			2	1		8
7	9		1		3	5		2
			9				6	

Puzzle 190

6				4			8	1
1		4			2			
7	3			1				9
8		5		7	1			
	7		4	5	9		2	
			3	8		7		4
9				2			4	7
			9			5		3
5	1			3				2

Answers on Page 277

Puzzle 191

					1		8	
				6	5	7		
			2	4	9	6		5
8	3		4			9	7	
6	4	1				3	5	2
	7	9			3		6	4
9		7	6	1	4			
		4	5	9				
	1		7					

Puzzle 192

1				4		8	3	
9	3		2		1	7		
	5	7						2
	9	3	7				2	
	7				8	4	6	
2						9	7	
		9	1		5		8	6
	6	1		9				4

Puzzle 193

9			2				8	
2				1		4	6	
1		4		3				
	2	7	9	5		1		
8	4						5	6
		5		6	7	2	4	
				8		6		4
	3	6		9				2
	8				1			5

Puzzle 194

		4	3	1	5	9	6	7
						4		
		7	4				3	
	8	1		2				
5	7		1	8	6		4	3
				9		1	5	
	9				7	6		
		3						
2	1	8	6	5	9	3		

Answers on Page 278

				8		7	5	
4	7	6		5	1		8	
	8		3				2	
						1	4	7
	3		4		5		6	
7	6	4						
	5				9		1	
	4		8	1		6	9	5
	9	2		4				

	7				3	6	8	
1	4		8					
	8			6			7	4
		5			8			9
8			6		7			2
2			3			1		
4	5			1			2	
					5		1	7
	3	1	4				9	

Puzzle 197

			3					7
		8	5	7		2	3	1
3				4				9
	6	5					7	
4	7		2	1	8		5	6
	9					3	4	
9				6				4
2	8	4		9	3	6		
7					1			

Puzzle 198

					1		2	9
4	9	8	3	2			6	
					8	7		
8	3	5	2			4	9	7
9	4	6			5	2	1	8
		9	1					
	1			9	3	6	5	2
2	8		6					

Answers on Page 278

9	7							2
8				4				
	6	1	3			4	8	9
	4		9	3		8		
2		9	7		4	1		6
		5		8	6		9	
6	5	2			1	9	4	
				6				5
3							2	8

7		5					1	
2	6		7			9		
3	8		9	2			4	
	2			7				6
6	1		2		5		7	9
5				3			2	
	3			6	4		9	5
		9			7		6	4
	7					1		3

Puzzle 201

		1			7			
	3			5	9			
9		7	8					4
4	9		5	3				
3		8	9		2	6		5
				1	6		9	3
7					1	4		2
			6	2			1	
			7			9		

Puzzle 202

		7			6	2		
	6			7		8		
4		9	1					5
	1	6	4			3		7
8		4				6		9
9		3			2	4	5	
3					1	9		6
		1		9			8	
		8	3			1		

Answers on Page 278

Puzzle 203

8			9	2	1		7	
7	2				5		3	
			3		7		1	
	7	5	6		3		9	
	9		7		4	3	8	
	8		4		9			
	5		1				4	9
	6		2	3	8			1

Puzzle 204

6		1		7	8			4
		3		2	9			8
2	9		5			7		
	4		9	6			7	
		9				4		
	2			5	4		1	
		7			2		4	5
3			4	1		9		
5			8	9		6		3

Puzzle 205

			1	7	3		6	5
	7							
2			4	6				
7		9	2	8			5	
4		2		9		8		7
	8			4	7	9		3
				5	2			4
							8	
5	9		8	3	6			

Puzzle 206

					7		2	
4		7	3			6		
2	3				4	1		
7		5	9		6		4	
		2		4		5		
	4		5		8	9		1
		3	1				8	9
		1			9	2		3
	9		2					

Answers on Page 279

Puzzle 207

		2	1					8
9			7		2	5		
		1	9				7	4
			5	8		6		2
		6	3	1	4	7		
7		5		9	6			
5	4				9	1		
		3	6		5			7
6					1	3		

Puzzle 208

		9	6		7	8	1	5
				8		6		
6			4					
		2		4	9	3	7	1
	3						4	
5	7	4	2	3		9		
					6			8
		7		5				
1	8	6	3		4	2		

Puzzle 209

5	6				8		1	9
		8				2	3	
7			5	1				
	7	1			2			
	3		9	8	4		7	
			1			3	4	
				4	6			3
	1	6				4		
9	2		3				8	6

Puzzle 210

	6	4			5	1	2	
8	5				4			6
3							9	
	1		9		6	5	4	
			5	4	8			
	4	9	3		2		8	
	2							4
1			4				6	9
	9	7	8			2	5	

Answers on Page 279

1	2			5			3	9
4		5				2		8
						7		
2	5		3	6			9	
	8	1				4	6	
	9			4	1		8	2
		8						
9		2				5		1
5	4			9			2	6

			7	1	2	6		
	5	2	4		9		7	
1	7					2	8	
			9	5				2
	8		2		3		5	
2				4	7			
	2	6					1	7
	9		6		5	3	2	
		7	1	2	8			

Puzzle 213

			8				5	
9			7	2	5	8		
		1	6	4				
6		9		7		1	2	3
		7		6		5		
5	2	8		3		7		9
				8	6	4		
		5	4	9	7			1
	7				1			

Puzzle 214

9					8	6		7
	1	6		7			9	
5	4	7			6		8	
	7		3	6				
6		5				2		4
				2	5		7	
	2		6			7	1	5
	6			4		3	2	
3		1	7					8

Answers on Page 279

	7	3	4				2	
	1			9		7		
9		6	7	8	2			1
		4					3	9
1				2				6
6	3					5		
4			2	6	7	8		3
		9		5			4	
	2				4	6	1	

		1				6	2	9
5							7	8
	3		2		6			5
1		4	7					6
2	8		5		9		3	1
9					1	2		4
4			8		5		6	
3	1							7
6	9	5				8		

Puzzle 217

5		3	2	7		6	1	
	9	2				4		
		7	8	1		2		
	1	4	7					
3				4				8
					2	1	4	
		6		8	1	7		
		9				5	6	
	4	1		9	5	8		2

Puzzle 218

		8		3				2
			6			7	3	
3	7		1					5
	3	2	4				6	9
			7	1	3			
1	8				9	3	7	
5					6		4	3
	9	7			5			
4				2		9		

Answers on Page 280

Puzzle 219

		9			4			
8			1				3	2
	6	1		7	8	9		
9	3			4			8	
		6	5		1	7		
	7			2			6	4
		8	4	5		1	7	
6	1				7			3
			6			4		

Puzzle 220

				9			6	
			2					1
6			4		8	3	5	7
5	3		1		9		7	2
2	9						8	5
1	6		5		2		4	3
9	5	2	7		3			6
8					6			
	7			2				

Answers on Page 280

Answers on Page 280

Puzzle 221

		1	8	4				5
3					7		4	
7				9	1	2		
5					4		3	9
6		9				1		4
4	3		6					8
		6	9	8				7
	9		1					2
1				3	2	8		

Puzzle 222

	5							
3	9				2	7	4	
7		6	3	1	4	9		
		3		7		8		
	1		9		8		5	
		9		6		1		
		4	5	9	6	2		8
	6	7	8				1	4
							3	

		1	5	4	2			
6		2			3	1		7
				6	1		4	
5	3	7						
		9	2	8	5	4		
						9	1	5
	8		9	5				
9		6	1			5		4
			3	7	6	8		

	8	3	5		9			
1	7	9		3				
	2	6	8				4	3
	6	5				1		7
				2				
2		1				6	9	
7	1				2	5	6	
				1		4	3	2
			6		5	7	1	

Puzzle 225

8						6	4	9
			9					
4		6		8	3	7		1
1		8					7	
9		3		1		8		2
	7					1		4
2		1	7	9		3		6
					2			
3	8	4						7

Puzzle 226

9		7	8				2	5
	5		6	9		1		
			3	7			9	8
		4				9	3	2
7	3	1				8		
5	1			2	6			
		3		4	1		7	
4	7				8	2		9

Answers on Page 280

Puzzle 227

			8	6		5		
9	7					6	2	1
			9		1	3	4	8
					5	4	8	9
8	2	5	6					
7	6	1	5		4			
4	8	3					7	5
		2		1	7			

Puzzle 228

	9	2		1	5	6		3
5	6		4	8			1	9
				2			8	
			2				3	
	4		1		8		7	
	7				4			
	2			7				
7	1			9	2		6	8
9		3	5	4		7	2	

Puzzle 229

7						1	3	
		2		4		6	8	9
	9		6				5	
		5		6	9			1
		9	7	5	4	8		
3			8	1		9		
	2				6		4	
8	6	7		9		3		
	4	1						6

Puzzle 230

	5		3	4		8		2
							6	
6				1		4	7	5
1			7	6			9	
			2		5			
	9			3	1			6
5	6	4		2				7
	2							
7		3		5	9		4	

Answers on Page 281

				2				
2	7						8	
5	3				9			6
	4	8		5	3		1	
9	1		4		7		3	2
	6		1	9		7	5	
1			7				6	5
	8						4	7
				3				

2			3	7			6	
6		8	2		9	1		
	3	9		6				
1			8	4		2		
			5		2			
		5		1	6			8
				3		4	8	
		6	4			5		9
	9			2	5			3

Puzzle 233

		9					8	2
2						9	1	6
	8		6			3		
1	5	9	8	3	7		6	
			5		9			
	2		4	6	1	8	9	5
		7			6		3	
4	3	6						9
5	1				3			

Puzzle 234

2	4				8		9	6
6	7			9			2	
			2		3	4	5	7
9		7				5	3	
	2	6				9		1
4	6	2	3		9			
	1			8			6	4
7	5		6				1	9

Answers on Page 281

Puzzle 235

7		9		8		5		
5	4		6			3		9
		6					2	
6			7				9	2
	9	1	4		6	7	5	
2	3				5			8
	6					2		
9		5			3		8	1
		2		1		9		6

Puzzle 236

4		3		2			5	6
	6	2				9		
7				5		4	2	
		6	5	9				
9	3	4				6	1	5
				3	4	8		
	7	1		6				9
		8				2	6	
6	9			8		3		1

Puzzle 237

		5		9			2	6
		9				8	1	
1			3					7
9				3		7	8	
3		8	4	1	2	5		9
	2	6		8				3
6					9			1
	1	3				6		
8	9			6		2		

Puzzle 238

8					2			
		2		9		4		1
1	3	6		5				9
		7		3	1			
	4		8		7		9	
			9	4		2		
5				7		6	4	2
4		9		6		5		
			5					3

Answers on Page 281

Puzzle 239

6						9		4
		4		2			5	
	2		4	6	5	8		3
			1	9			3	2
2		1				7		6
4	3			8	7			
1		5	6	4	2		7	
	4			5		1		
9		7						5

Puzzle 240

	2	1	5		9	6		3
4	5			7	6			
	9			4		7	5	2
1	4	2						
						4	6	1
6	1	9		2			8	
			1	3			9	6
5		8	6		7	1	2	

Puzzle 241

4		1						
				7	8	3		
		8	5	6			7	4
9	4		1				3	
1	3						5	2
	8				6		4	9
2	9			1	7	5		
		7	6	3				
						2		7

Puzzle 242

7							1	
		9	2		5			4
4		6	7					
	2		5	3				
1	3						5	7
				7	2		8	
					7	6		8
5			6		1	3		
	7							1

Answers on Page 282

Puzzle 243

	2						6	7
			4		7	3		
5			1	6		2		
8				4				
		1	8	3	9	4		
				7				3
		8		9	5			2
		9	7		6			
1	6						3	

Puzzle 244

4			6		8	5		
8	2	5	1					
		7						8
	8			3				1
	3		2		6		9	
9				1			3	
1						9		
					1	7	8	6
		8	4		7			3

Puzzle 245

	8	2	5		4	1		3
		3	1				6	5
					3			4
5	2	7						
						8	5	7
1			4					
2	3				8	5		
7		8	6		5	9	2	

Puzzle 246

		9		8			5	
		3						
		5	3		4	9	8	2
5				4	3			
	2	8		6		7	3	
			8	2				6
3	5	6	4		9	8		
						6		
	8			5		4		

Answers on Page 282

		3			5			1
1					2			
7			9		1		6	
4		1			6		2	
9								6
	6		1			8		3
	1		2		9			7
			7					5
5			8			6		

	8		4			2		
		5		2		9		
9				7		4	1	
	1	2	8				5	6
			3		2			
3	4				7	8	2	
	9	8		3				2
		1		6		5		
		4			5		3	

Puzzle 249

4			7					
		8		6			4	5
1	3			2	4			
7			2					6
	9			7			3	
5					1			7
			4	5			8	3
8	1			9		6		
					2			9

Puzzle 250

	6			7			8	
	7				2			
					3		7	2
		8			6		2	
4	3		5		8		6	9
	9		4			5		
6	4		2					
			3				5	
	2			5			1	

Answers on Page282

Puzzle 251

	7		1	5				
		2		3				6
4	1	6						
		1	9				2	
2		9	3		1	4		8
	6				5	3		
						9	3	2
1				2		7		
				8	3		4	

Puzzle 252

	6		1				7	
7							4	9
	8			9		6		
				2	6	9		
5	3	2		8		7	1	6
		7	3	1				
		5		4			9	
8	2							7
	4				2		3	

Puzzle 253

2	1		6	7		3	5	
				5		6		2
	5				4			
				2		9		7
	3	7				5	2	
5		2		1				
			5				8	
9		1		3				
	4	5		8	1		9	3

Puzzle 254

				7	3			2
2			8				4	5
		4					1	
3			7	4			6	1
			6		1			
9	1			2	8			7
	8					5		
1	3				9			4
7			5	8				

Answers on Page 283

Puzzle 255

	3	1			9		2	
			3					6
8	2							
6			9	1		7		
4	7						5	8
		2		7	8			3
							3	4
9					3			
	6		5			9	8	

Puzzle 256

				4				
	6		8			3		7
1				9	6			5
	7	4			9			2
			2	6	5			
2			4			1	3	
4			6	2				3
8		2			4		7	
				7				

Puzzle 257

3								
	5	1	9					6
2					5	3		7
				9	6		4	
		5	4		3	6		
	8		2	5				
5		4	3					2
1					9	7	6	
								4

Puzzle 258

1		5	2		6			
7							2	
		6	4	7				
	2	8						9
6	1						3	5
3						1	4	
			4	8	6			
	5							4
			9		7	3		1

Answers on Page 283

				4	9		2	
	7			2	3		5	4
2				7				
						3		6
	9	4	7		2	5	8	
3		8						
				8				5
8	2		3	1			7	
	3		4	9				

3	5			1				6
7	4	9	5			1		
	1			8			9	
				6	3	9		
			4		5			
		4	8	2				
	3			5			6	
		1			8	5	3	7
8				9			1	2

Puzzle 261

4			5	9		8		
5			3				6	
8	3	6		7				
7	4		8	3				
		5				3		
				6	5		4	2
				5		4	2	1
	7				3			6
		2		4	9			8

Puzzle 262

7	3	6						9
				5			7	
					9	4		6
					1		5	
	5	2	6	7	3	8	4	
	1		8					
2		4	9					
	9			1				
6						9	2	8

Answers on Page 283

Puzzle 263

				7	9			8
	9	5	1			6		
	4	7			2			
5		2					8	
		4				3		
	3					9		7
			7			5	2	
		3			4	8	1	
6			9	8				

Puzzle 264

	8	9	5					4
		2		6				
6	5	7	3					
				3		4	7	9
5	7	6		9				
					3	6	8	7
				4		5		
3					7	1	4	

Puzzle 265

			4		2			
	2						6	4
7			6	3			9	
	4	3						8
1			5		4			2
2						9	4	
	6			7	8			5
4	1						2	
			9		1			

Puzzle 266

	7	9	1					
4	6	8					7	2
						6		
			6	2		7		5
	2			7			1	
7		4		3	8			
		2						
6	9					4	8	3
					5	2	6	

Answers on Page 284

Puzzle 267

2		9			4	8		
						1		
			3	6	9	4	2	
4		1				3	7	6
	5						1	
9	3	2				5		4
	9	8	5	2	7			
		4						
		5	8			7		3

Puzzle 268

8	4	1	5					3
			6	4		8		9
	5	9	3					
	6					1	8	
9								7
	8	7					3	
					3	5	4	
4		3		1	5			
5					6	3	7	2

Puzzle 269

6			9					
1						6	7	
	3		8			4		9
		1	2	6				7
		6		4		5		
5				1	9	3		
9		7			4		2	
	2	3						6
					2			4

Puzzle 270

5		3	6	8		9		
7					5			4
	6							
	2		4		9	1		
1								5
		8	2		1		4	
							5	
4			8					9
		7		2	4	6		3

Answers on Page 284

Puzzle 271

		7	3					6
8				7				
6	1						7	
	2		6	5				8
1		3				9		2
7				9	3		1	
	9						2	7
				1				5
5					7	4		

Puzzle 272

	6	8		1	4	7		2
				9				8
7	2				8		5	
			6				2	
2		6				8		9
	1				7			
	8		9				7	4
6				2				
1		3	4	7		2	8	

PUZZLE 273

5					9		2	6
		9		8				
	6					9		1
				5	4			3
7		1	3	6	8	2		5
3			7	2				
1		3					4	
				7		1		
9	8		6					7

Puzzle 274

5		4			2			
	3				8	4		
	1		7				2	5
6		7		1		8		
1								9
		3		8		7		1
4	5				9		7	
		2	5				4	
			6			5		3

Answers on Page 284

Puzzle 275

				6			7	9
		1			2			4
		8	5					
		6		8	3		2	
8		5		2		6		7
	9		6	7		1		
					4	9		
6			7			2		
4	8			5				

Puzzle 276

			6	2		4		
		2				6		
7			4		1	5		2
		7			4	8		
	2		7		3		4	
		3	8			7		
1		4	9		5			6
		6				9		
		8		1	6			

Puzzle 277

		7		2	8		9	5
			7			1		
3		6	5		9			
4				9			5	6
	6						8	
8	9			3				1
			1		2	6		9
		2			4			
6	1		9	8		5		

Puzzle 278

			7	9	2	4		
		8		4				3
9	6							
	7			6	8		4	
		6	2		7	8		
	1		4	5			9	
							5	1
6				7		2		
		1	3	2	4			

Answers on Page 285

```
. . . | . . 9 | . 4 2
8 3 . | . . . | . 9 1
. 9 . | 6 . 8 | . . 3
------+-------+------
. . . | 1 . . | . . .
. 1 5 | . 6 . | 2 7 .
. . . | . . 3 | . . .
------+-------+------
4 . . | 7 . 6 | . 2 .
1 6 . | . . . | . 3 7
7 8 . | 9 . . | . . .
```

```
2 . . | 3 7 . | . . .
7 . 1 | 6 . . | 3 5 .
. 8 . | . 4 . | . . 6
------+-------+------
6 9 . | . 3 . | . . .
. . . | 2 . 1 | . . .
. . . | . 9 . | . 3 4
------+-------+------
8 . . | . 1 . | . 4 .
. 2 4 | . . 7 | 9 . 5
. . . | . 5 3 | . . 7
```

Puzzle 281

	9		2			5	3	
	4		9				8	6
			1				4	9
				7		4	6	
	8		3		5		9	
	7	2		6				
7	6				1			
9	5				3		1	
	2	1			8		7	

Puzzle 282

2	3		4		1			7
					5		1	2
			2			8		
	7				4		8	6
			7					
9	4		5				7	
		6			3			
4	2		8					
3			1		9		4	5

Answers on Page 285

Twisted

Puzzle 283

	4			3				5
7	3	2				4		
9				4		6		2
			5	9	4		2	7
2	8		7	1	6			
1		3		7				8
		4				2	6	1
8				5			9	

Puzzle 284

4	8			3		9		7
	7			4	8			
	9	3			1			
2		4			6		7	
		5					4	
	3		5			1		6
			4			7	8	
			7	6			9	
3		7		1			6	5

Answers on Page 285

Page 149

Puzzle 285

9				1					3
	7							4	
		4			7		6		2
7			8	4	2			1	6
					7				
2	3		9	5	6				7
6		7	5				9		
	1							2	
8					9				4

Puzzle 286

9	6								
5					7	6	8		
7				4	9			1	
				5			2		
1		8	6		2	9		7
		5				9			
	4				5	7			8
		9	8	3					4
								9	5

Answers on Page 285

Puzzle 287

6					3	8		
4			9				5	6
7	2			8				
					7		9	8
	6			4			7	
2	5		1					
				5			1	4
5	8				9			7
		4	7					5

Puzzle 288

6	2				3	7	4	8
4					7			5
		8		4			6	
				2	5		3	
		4					5	
	5		8	1				
	3			5		8		
8			2					1
1	4	5	7				2	9

Puzzle 289

		8		4			3	6
		9						
				3	1	8		
7		2		1				5
		6	8	7	5	2		
4				2		9		1
		4	2	9				
						5		
6	9			5		3		

Puzzle 290

				2				
	1	5			7			
	9			1		3	8	6
	7	9		8		5		4
5								8
4		3		9		1	6	
9	6	1		7			2	
			2			8	1	
				5				

Answers on Page 286

Puzzle 291

				9		4		
		2	1		4	8	3	6
			5					
	4		8	2		3		
1		8				6		5
		7		1	5		4	
					1			
6	8	3	9		7	1		
		5		8				

Puzzle 292

								8
			9	8	7	6		
	1	8			3		2	
	2					8		
1	9		8	6	2		4	7
		3					5	
	7		6			2	9	
		2	7	1	9			
9								

Puzzle 293

7		8		4			9	
4				8	3			
	2	3	9					
8				1			3	7
	6						8	
2	1			5				4
					6	4	5	
			5	3				9
	3			2		6		1

Puzzle 294

			2		5	3	9	
						6		7
	4		6		3			
	3	6	7	1				5
		1	5		4	9		
5				6	2	7	3	
			4		7		2	
4		7						
	5	9	3		6			

Answers on Page 286

Puzzle 295

	1		6	5		3		8
3			7		4	5		
			9			1		
8		5					9	
7			5		9			3
	9					4		2
		6			3			
		3	2		5			4
5		2		9	6		3	

Puzzle 296

	4			7	9		2	
						8		
					2	6	3	9
7			4			9		
	3	2		6		4	8	
		5			3			7
2	9	4	7					
		7						
	1		6	5			9	

Puzzle 297

8						1		7
	5	3						2
		2	8					
	4				8	3		1
	8		6	9	1		2	
1		9	4				8	
					5	6		
6						9	7	
5		1						3

Puzzle 298

		2	8		7	3		4
	4						8	
8					5			
				1			6	7
7	5			2			1	8
9	1			5				
			1					5
	8						3	
2		9	5		3	4		

Answers on Page 286

Puzzle 299

		3			4			
	9						3	
6	4				8		9	5
2			7			8	1	
8				9				4
	3	1			2			9
9	7		8				5	2
	2						6	
			2			7		

Puzzle 300

2								
	4	5	1	2				7
			8	5				2
5		8	4					
9	1			3			8	4
					7	9		3
1				6	8			
4				9	5	6	3	
								8

Puzzle 301

7		3	8		1		5	2
5					4			
		4	3			8		
					7			
8	7						4	1
			6					
		5			3	6		
			1					4
1	4		2		5	3		9

Puzzle 302

4	1		8		5	9	3	
	5		7					1
	3							8
					9			
	2		4	1	7		8	
			2					
6							5	
8					1		2	
	9	2	5		3		4	6

Answers on Page 287

Puzzle 303

	9					5		
		7						1
6	2	4	1		7			8
	5		6			8		
7			9		4			6
		3			5		2	
9			7		2	1	8	3
3						7		
		8					4	

Puzzle 304

6		4		8	9			
						8	5	6
		5		6				
2	9	7					4	1
		6		1		9		
1	4					2	6	8
				4		1		
5	3	9						
			9	5		3		2

Puzzle 305

	4	9		1	5	7		
		7			4			
3		6					5	4
7				2	9		1	
	6		7	3				9
6	3					8		2
			6			5		
		2	8	4		1	7	

Puzzle 306

	3	4	6					
2				3				
8					1		9	5
		7		5	9		3	
		3				7		
	1		7	6		5		
3	4		1					7
				9				6
					4	1	8	

Answers on Page 287

Puzzle 307

		8		4		1		
			1				6	4
			5					7
8		1	4	3		9		
	5		6	9	1		7	
		7		2	5	4		3
3					9			
9	8				4			
		5		8		7		

Puzzle 308

			5	9			8	3
				3				
3	9	1						4
	5				4			
6	4		9		8		1	5
			3				6	
9						6	5	2
				4				
2	8			7	9			

Answers on Page 287

Puzzle 309

5		6	4				3	
8	1				2			4
7		4			6	5		
				2	1		5	
1								6
	7		5	8				
		8	1			4		3
3			2				6	5
	5				4	7		9

Puzzle 310

9		6	2				4	3
		7		4	8		2	
						1		
7					3		5	
5		9	6		4	2		1
	1		5					7
		1						
	9		7	6		4		
2	7				1	8		9

Answers on Page 287

Puzzle 311

				1	6		4	
			9					
3	6	1					8	
2	4	3	6	9	5			
8			2		1			4
			8	4	3	5	2	6
	3					4	1	9
					9			
	8		4	5				

Puzzle 312

	1	5	8			3		
		8					6	4
6	7							
2	3	4	9				8	
			6		3			
	5				2	4	3	9
							2	7
3	8					9		
		7			8	5	4	

Puzzle 313

7					3		2	6
	8	3	5				1	
6								5
8	6			5	7			
	4			3			7	
			1	6			5	2
9								8
	2				5	7	3	
1	7		3					4

Puzzle 314

	5	9	2			3		
1		7			3			
2						9		6
6					8			
	4		5	1	9		3	
			3					7
5		4						3
			9			4		8
		2			4	7	6	

Answers on Page 288

Puzzle 315

8					1			
	2				6	1		
		7			5	8		4
		5	6	2		7		9
		2	1		8	6		
6		8		9	7	2		
4		1	8			9		
		6	3				1	
			7					6

Puzzle 316

	7				5			
2		5	9		4			3
			2				7	8
3		7			1	8	6	4
9	1	4	6			2		7
4	3				8			
8			4		7	3		5
			3				8	

Puzzle 317

			2	4				
		1	8		9			5
			6		7		4	8
8	2			6				
5	6						9	4
				2			8	6
9	1		7		6			
2			3		5	7		
				9	2			

Puzzle 318

5	9		2			3		
				4		7	1	
6					8		9	
4	7		9		6			2
9			8		3		4	1
	6		3					7
	5	9		8				
		3			1		2	9

Answers on Page 288

Puzzle 319

```
. 5 . | 2 . . | . . .
8 6 3 | . 1 7 | . 4 5
7 . . | . . 3 | . . .
------+-------+------
5 . 6 | . . . | . 7 1
. . . | . 6 . | . . .
2 1 . | . . . | 4 . 6
------+-------+------
. . . | 3 . . | . . 9
1 9 . | 6 4 . | 8 3 7
. . . | . . 8 | . 1 .
```

Puzzle 320

```
. . 4 | 7 . 3 | . . .
. . 5 | . . . | . . .
9 7 . | . 5 1 | . . 3
------+-------+------
. . 7 | . 3 . | 5 6 2
. . . | . . . | . . .
2 6 3 | . 8 . | 9 . .
------+-------+------
6 . . | 3 1 . | . 9 8
. . . | . . . | 2 . .
. . . | 4 . 5 | 7 . .
```

Answers on Page 288

Puzzle 321

	2					3		
					1	6		4
6		1	9			5		8
	6	9	7			8		
	8		5		6		3	
		4			8	2	1	
5		6			9	7		2
4		8	6					
		3					6	

Puzzle 322

	7			5			3	
		6		8	3		2	9
	2	9			6			
2							1	6
		7		3		9		
1	9							3
			3			8	7	
8	4		1	7		3		
	3			2			9	

Answers on Page 288

Puzzle 323

			9		8			
3		8			4			5
		4	6		9	1	2	
7	1	5		8				
		6			5	4	1	
5	8	4		1	6			
6		1			7			4
		3		8				

Puzzle 324

	5			1				9
6	3		4	2				
					5		4	
		8	5				3	
	7	6		8		2	9	
	9				7	1		
	2		6					
				5	3		2	1
1				7			6	

Answers on Page 288

Answers on Page 289

Puzzle 325

2	3		1	8	9			
	6							5
			6		5			
	7	2			3	9		1
	4		8		2		5	
3		1	9			2	4	
			5		4			
7							9	
			7	9	8		3	4

Puzzle 326

		5	7					
6	3	1			2			
2	7			1			5	9
5	4		8					
7			6		9			5
					3		1	7
9	5			8			3	1
			1			2	7	8
					7	5		

Answers on Page 289

Puzzle 327

					1			
	4	1		6				2
9						1		8
	1			9	2		7	6
		9				2		
8	7		5	4			9	
7		4						3
3				2		4	8	
			9					

Puzzle 328

				8	2		9	
6			5		3			7
2	3			4		6		
	5				6	4		
		3				7		
		6	9				3	
		7		9			6	1
1			8		5			3
	6		3	7				

Page 171

Puzzle 329

		6				7	2	9
	2		1	7			4	
	3				6			
2			5			9	1	
	4			1			6	
	5	1			9			8
			9				5	
	9			3	8		7	
8	6	2				3		

Puzzle 330

4					9		3	2
		6			3			1
					7	5	8	
	8	4						
1	9			7			2	6
						8	9	
	4	1	7					
8			9			4		
5	3		1					8

Answers on Page 289

Puzzle 331

		3		9		2		8
7		8					6	
	2	5			8			
	6		9	4				3
				3				
3				2	6		9	
			3			5	7	
	3					4		2
4		1		7		8		

Puzzle 332

					7	8	4	
6		2			3			
		7	4					2
2					6	5		8
5	7						6	3
1		6	3					4
4				5		9		
			8			4		1
	9	8	1					

Puzzle 333

2			7					8
	9					1	3	
	4		9	1		6		7
			4					3
5			6	8	9			1
4					1			
3		5		7	4		1	
	8	4					2	
6					5			4

Puzzle 334

		1		5	3	4		
	7						6	1
			1	2				9
			3	9		6		
2		9		4		3		5
		7		1	6			
3				6	4			
7	9						4	
		4	2	7		9		

Answers on Page 289

3	1	7			6			
	6							
9			3			1	6	4
		1		3	9	2		
	7		1		5		9	
		9	6	4		7		
1	8	2			7			5
							7	
			5			9	8	1

				4		5		
6	8		5					3
9			7			8		4
8				7				5
		7	2	3	4	6		
3				1				7
4		6			1			8
1					9		3	2
		8		5				

Puzzle 337

4					5			3
	8			9				
	1			4	8	5		
1		6	9	2		4		
			5	8	4			
		4		3	1	7		9
		7	4	5			3	
				1			9	
5			8					4

Puzzle 338

				7	1	4		
					4		7	5
		4		5			3	
1				4	3	6	9	
		8				2		
	5	6	2	1				3
	3			2		9		
8	2		6					
		5	4	8				

Answers on Page 290

Puzzle 339

5			7			2		
1				5		4		
	6	8			3		7	5
					6			
3		7		9		5		6
			3					
6	2		1			7	4	
		4		7				2
		1			2			9

Puzzle 340

	4							1
7		1	9	4	5			
	6	3		1				9
						2		
3	2			5			8	4
		7						
2				7		6	1	
			8	6	2	7		3
8							9	

Answers on Page 290

Puzzle 341

3				2				7
6	1				7			
4				9			6	
		2	8			6		4
			6	4	3			
8		4			2	5		
	5			3				6
			1				9	8
9				6				5

Puzzle 342

		2		9		4		5
5			1	7		3	9	6
		3					7	
			4				3	
		5		1		6		
	6				8			
	7					5		
1	5	8		6	7			3
3		9		8		2		

Answers on Page 290

3		8			1			6
			8					
	9	5			3	4		
5	7					2	8	
9								7
	8	3					6	9
		1	9			3	5	
					7			
8			3			6		2

		1	2		6		9	
		2			5			3
4		7				5	2	1
	1			2		3		
2								6
		3		8			5	
8	2	9				1		7
5			1			6		
	3		7		2	9		

Puzzle 345

4	6				1	7		8
			8					
	8	9					1	
	9	1		4			6	
		6		9		1		
	5			6		4	8	
	7					5	3	
					4			
2		4	7				9	6

Puzzle 346

					9		7	
		8					4	5
			8	7	2		3	
	1	3		2				9
	2	7		9		5		1
9				6		3	8	
	8		9	1	3			
7	9					4		
	6		2					

Answers on Page 290

		8						9
5	6				4			
4			1	2				
		2		1	8	3	7	
7	3			4			8	1
	8	4	9	3		2		
				8	6			5
			4				3	8
8						4		

		7	2					
9		6			1			4
3			8		9	1		5
	6	3	5					
	4			1			2	
					8	6	5	
2		8	4		6			7
6			1			8		9
					5	3		

Puzzle 349

				2	8			
	4	7			9			
	3						8	9
3			8				4	1
4	1			6			9	3
5	6				3			7
1	8						3	
			7			4	5	
			3	5				

Puzzle 350

		7					2	8
			7		2			
2		1	9	3			7	6
			4				3	1
	7			2			8	
1	9				8			
9	3			1	6	8		7
			8		3			
6	1					5		

Answers on Page 291

Puzzle 351

Puzzle 352

Puzzle 353

6					4	3		7
3	5			7	9			
7		1			6			
2						1	5	9
		8				2		
1	6	4						3
			6			9		1
			7	8			4	2
4		3	9					8

Puzzle 354

	1		6				5	
	3	7	2			9		
		5				4		2
			4	6				1
5		6		1		2		7
1				5	7			
8		1				3		
		4			1	7	9	
	9				8		6	

Answers on Page 291

Puzzle 355

	8		2		6			
6					5	9		2
				4			7	1
		9	8				2	3
		4		2		1		
2	1				9	8		
3	9			6				
4		6	5					8
			4		2		9	

Puzzle 356

			2		4			
4	6						2	
	9			3	6			7
8						3	4	
2			4		5			1
	4	9						2
5			8	7			6	
	2						1	4
			1		9			

Puzzle 357

2					6	3		
	6				7		4	1
3				4	1			
				6				4
		2				5		
8				9				
			1	7				8
9	8		6				2	
		1	3					5

Puzzle 358

				6			2	
5	3				2			
				5	4			
8	5	6				3		
2	9						4	8
		4				6	1	9
		3	9					
			2				8	1
	8			4				

Answers on Page 291

9				5			6	
8					9			
		6	8			7	9	
		1			8		2	
2				6				8
	8		1			5		
	4	5			7	2		
			5					7
	1			9				3

			1				5	6
4	9			6				
				2			7	
3	7							
	6	1	8	4	3	7	2	
							9	3
	5			9				
				8			1	4
2	4				6			

Puzzle 361

	3		5		1		9	
9	4		2					
8				7				
5							2	
	6		4		3		5	
	1							7
				8				1
					7		8	2
	8		1		4		3	

Puzzle 362

	3	9	7				6	8
8			4					
		5		8				
3		8				2	1	9
4	9	7				8		5
				4		3		
					9			6
5	1				7	9	2	

Answers on Page 292

	9			7	2			
7						2		1
4					8		6	
		3			9			
8		4	2		1	3		9
			6			5		
	5		1					6
1		8						3
			8	9			4	

7			4	5				
					1			2
2	3		6			8		
			1				9	
1		5				4		3
	7				4			
		1			3		8	9
6			5					
				1	6			7

Puzzle 365

	8	7		6	2			9
6								
		2	8		4	6		
								2
	7	8		5		9	3	
9								
		4	9		3	5		
								8
3			7	4		1	9	

Puzzle 366

7	6							8
			2				7	3
3	5		4				2	
			7			9		
			5	6	2			
		7			1			
	3				7		6	2
2	1				4			
9							8	1

Answers on Page 292

	4				5	6		
5		7				2	8	
1					7			
2	6	4				1		
				9				
		3				4	2	8
			3					5
	5	8				7		2
		1	8				4	

				6	3			2
6						3		
			4			5		7
		5		3				9
		8	9	4	5	2		
3				7		4		
7		6			8			
		1						4
9			2	5				

Puzzle 369

	8				3			
2		4		5				7
	3					8	6	4
			6				1	
1		2				4		9
	7				1			
7	2	3					9	
9				8		7		1
			9				5	

Puzzle 370

		4		3			2	
		3	4			1	9	
	1		9		8		5	
			1					
4		5				7		1
					5			
	4		5		9		8	
	6	9			4	2		
	8			2		4		

Answers on Page 292

4	7				6			2
				5			7	8
					4		1	
			3		8	1		
	9			4			8	
		4	2		1			
	3		4					
6	2			3				
7			1				6	3

3					7	2		
				8				3
	2	1			3		4	
1	8		9					4
	4						7	
6					4		5	2
	1		3			6	8	
5				6				
		6	2					1

Puzzle 373

								3
7	2	9	1					
				5		2	6	
	8	4				5		
3	5	7				4	2	6
		2				7	3	
	3	6		7				
					5	3	9	4
2								

Puzzle 374

2		3	8				9	
					4		6	8
1			6		5			7
	2							1
			7		3			
3							4	
8			5		9			6
9	1		4					
	5				1	4		9

9			2				5	
		5			1	7	6	
				9		2		1
	4		3		7			
		9				8		
			9		2		1	
5		6		4				
	9	7	6			5		
	3				8			7

	3	4						
					5			
2		9	3		8	5		7
4		7		2			5	
	2						3	
	5			7		6		9
6		1	7		2	9		5
			9					
						1	7	

Puzzle 377

							5	
	6		9			4		
4	5		8		2			
		6	3			8		5
2			1		7			9
5		4			8	2		
			7		1		6	2
		1			9		3	
	3							

Puzzle 378

	4	6	1					
				3	4	6		5
				2	6	3		
	3	8	4					
		2				4		
					1	8	7	
		7	3	1				
2		4	5	9				
					2	7	8	

Answers on Page 293

Puzzle 379

			9	3			7	1
2			1	6			9	
						5		
	2			3	8	1		
		1				2		
		3	9	1			6	
		6						
	9			5	6			7
5	8		7	4				

Puzzle 380

				4			7	
	5	1		7	8			
		7			5			6
		2					4	
6	8		3		4		1	9
	1					8		
4			9			2		
			8	3		4	5	
	7			1				

Puzzle 381

	6	2			3			
9								
	7	1	2			8		
4			7	8		1		
1			5		4			3
		5		3	9			2
		7			1	3	5	
								1
			3			4	6	

Puzzle 382

4			9			8	1	
	9			2				
	5	6			8			
	1	5						4
		4				2		
6						9	7	
			2			1	4	
				1			9	
	7	9			5			6

Puzzle 383

	8		2					
9								4
	3		1	9	4		8	6
8					6	5		
				8				
		7	4					8
6	1		9	7	8		2	
5								1
					2		4	

Puzzle 384

	1			6	7		5	
	6		1					4
				8			7	
3			6					7
		4		3		8		
9					5			3
	9			4				
7					9		8	
	8		7	2			3	

Puzzle 385

7	9			3				4
		1				6		
	8			4	1			
			7	1	9	5		
		8				7		
		7	8	5	6			
			5	7			6	
		2				8		
6				9			7	1

Puzzle 386

8			9	7	4			
9		4				2	3	
	7		6	3				
	1	5						2
3						5	8	
				1	6		7	
	8	7				1		6
			4	2	7			3

Puzzle 387

5	2							6
	9	6		3		5	8		
1				6		5		
			1	2				7
6				4	7			
		6		8				3
		8	6		3		4	5
4							7	8

Puzzle 388

	4		8	3				
9	8		1					
		2			6			
1	7			4		8		
5				1				4
		8		9			1	6
			9			7		
					3		2	5
				6	2		3	

Puzzle 389

	4		6					
5	6							4
			4		2			8
6	8			3		4		
	3			8			1	
		9		6			8	2
4			8		5			
3							4	7
					9		2	

Puzzle 390

			4		6			
4		6					7	
2		1						6
		9			2	5		1
		7	3		5	6		
6		5	9			3		
7						2		9
	9					1		8
			2		3			

	4	8		9				
	9		6					
3			8		2	9		
		9			4		2	
5	3						6	9
	7		3			1		
		7	1		6			2
					7		8	
				8		7	1	

2					7	5		
		7	1	5			9	
		3						8
			2		6			1
	2	9				4	6	
1			4		9			
5						8		
	3			2	8	1		
		6	5					7

Puzzle 393

	6	4					1	
	7			6	8			
		9	1				2	
						2	4	7
			8	4	5			
9	4	3						
	2				4	9		
			9	2			6	
	9					4	8	

Puzzle 394

	2			3	1			
		8	5	4				
1							7	
5				9	7			6
		4		1		2		
3			6	2				5
	6							8
				7	3	9		
			1	8			3	

	1	7	9			6		2
5		2				4		
9								
			5			2		7
	7	3				1	5	
6		9			7			
								8
		1				3		4
3		8			6	7	2	

3	4		1			5	2	
	1			9				
5			6					8
2						1		
7			8		2			4
		3						2
9					8			1
				6			5	
	2	5			9		3	7

Answers on Page 294

Puzzle 397

5						6		
	4				7	5	3	
1		8	9					
				4				5
3	9						7	2
4				7				
					8	2		7
	1	3	2				8	
		2						1

Puzzle 398

		8					7	
			2				4	5
		9				3		1
				5	7			
4	1		6		2		9	8
			8	4				
9		7				2		
8	6				5			
	3					1		

Answers on Page 295

Puzzle 399

1			7	4		2		
	4							9
5				2	1			
9		2				1		
		3		1		6		
		4				5		3
			1	3				2
7							8	
		1		5	2			7

Puzzle 400

7		6	3		5			
					1			
9						8		7
6					4	7		1
		7		5		3		
4		8	1					9
2		1						6
			7					
			4		6	1		3

Answers on Page 295

Puzzle 401

	5	1				2		
							6	7
		4	8			5		
	6		5		2			4
			6		3			
3			4		9		2	
		5			6	4		
7	2							
		6				9	1	

Puzzle 402

5				9	7	4		
		4	8		5			
8								
	4	8		1			3	
	2	3				5	1	
	7			4		8	9	
								6
			7		9	3		
		6	3	8				5

Answers on Page 295

Puzzle 403

	9						2	
		4	5	2	1			
1			6			5		
4				1	7	9		
		7	8	9				3
		5			4			1
			9	7	3	6		
	8						3	

Puzzle 404

			1			5	7	3
		3		2				
5	1				8	6		
8			5			4		7
2		1			3			5
		5	2				1	4
				5		8		
1	8	9			4			

Puzzle 405

2			5	4				
4		8			9	6		
					8		2	
3		5						
	9		4		1		3	
						8		5
	1		3					
		7	8			4		6
				9	5			2

Puzzle 406

	9	8		6				2
		6		4	7			
					9			
1		4					2	5
		7		5		9		
5	3					6		4
			3					
			1	8		5		
3				7		4	9	

Answers on Page 295

				2		1	4	6
1	2							
	9			3		5		
	5		2			6		
			6	1	4			
		2			9		7	
		5		9			3	
							1	8
9	1	7		4				

	8		1					5
	3	1	7					
		6		4		1	9	
5			9					2
1					2			3
	1	7		3		9		
					7	4	8	
4					9		3	

Puzzle 409

8	7			4	3			
	1	3		8				6
		5					3	
			1	3				8
				9				
6				2	8			
	4					7		
3				6		5	2	
			4	5			6	3

Puzzle 410

					7			
	5			2				8
2					6	7		
	2	1		3		9	8	
	6	4				2	7	
	8	5		7		6	1	
		9	5					1
6				8			4	
			7					

Answers on Page 296

Puzzle 411

		8		9			7	
9					3	8		
	2			8	4			
				4	8		5	
	4		2		7		3	
	3		9	5				
			5	7			4	
		1	4					6
	7			1		2		

Puzzle 412

6				9		8		
3								7
		4					2	5
		1		5			3	
4		9	8		1	5		6
	8			3		1		
1	7					2		
9								4
		5		6				9

Puzzle 413

Puzzle 414

Answers on Page 296

Puzzle 415

1	6		4			7		
		7					6	
				9	7	4		2
			7		9			
	3			5			7	
			1		2			
3		6	9	4				
	5					3		
		4			6		5	1

Puzzle 416

				1		2		
	9				3		8	
3		1			9			4
	4		9					2
		5		8		7		
7					2		4	
4			3			8		5
	3		7				1	
		8		2				

Answers on Page 296

Puzzle 417

8		2			7			
			2		1			
	4		3					9
	7				5		4	6
		6		7		9		
3	5		1					2
9					2		1	
			7		4			
			6			8		3

Puzzle 418

			2	7		6		
					5	1		7
				4		3		2
6	2		1					
9				3				5
				8			7	6
3		2		1				
5		8	7					
		1		9	3			

Answers on Page 296

Puzzle 419

			2				9	
			7	8				4
	3			1	9	7		
1			8					7
		4		5		1		
3					1			9
		2	1	6			7	
9				7	5			
	5				8			

Puzzle 420

5			7			2		6
			1			9		
3				4			7	8
	5			8	4			
		6				5		
			5	1			8	
1	2			3				9
		5			9			
6		8			1			3

Puzzle 421

				6	4			9
		7		3		4		8
						3	2	
				8			3	
2		9				6		7
	6			7				
	9	8						
6		1		9		7		
4			6	5				

Puzzle 422

7	3						9	
2			8		6	5		1
6								
		4	3	9		7		
				4				
		3		6	2	1		
								5
1		7	2		9			3
	9						7	6

Answers on Page 297

Puzzle 423

	1	2	3			8	9	
				8	7		5	1
	4							
							8	4
		5				7		
4	2							
							1	
3	8		5	2				
	5	7			9	3	6	

Puzzle 424

		9	3		2			7
	5		9	4		1		
							6	9
	2				8			1
				7				
5			2			7		
8	3							
		4		1	9		3	
9			4		6	2		

Puzzle 425

			1	8				
4						8		
	8		6		3	2		
	4		8		1	5	2	
1								9
	2	3	7		5		1	
		9	5		4		3	
		6						4
				1	6			

Puzzle 426

							4	
				1	5	9		
7		5					3	6
5					2		1	4
	3		5		1		7	
4	8		9					3
6	5					4		1
		4	8	3				
	7							

Answers on Page 297

Puzzle 427

	1	7	3				9	6
		8	9					
4					2		5	
	4						8	
9				4				5
	5						4	
	3		1					8
					3	9		
8	2				5	6	3	

Puzzle 428

			4	9	5			8
				7				6
	2				3		4	
7				8			6	
		4	5		1	2		
	6			4				9
	1		9				7	
9				5				
5			7	3	4			

Puzzle 429

		1	4		7	3		
7				6				2
5	8			2		7		
			3				9	
		7				5		
	9				4			
		5		4			7	3
2				7				9
		9	5		8	2		

Puzzle 430

4					6	5		
	6		3					
1	9	3		2				
8		7	9					
5				6				2
					2	3		8
				1		8	9	4
					4		3	
		8	6					1

Answers on Page 297

Puzzle 431

6		1				5		
	4			2				8
	7			9	5			
	9	7	2			1		
		4				8		
		2			8	3	4	
			1	5			8	
9				6			3	
		6				9		1

Puzzle 432

			3			2	6	
								9
		8			2	1	7	
		1		8	7			4
3			4		5			1
2			9	3		5		
	5	3	1			7		
1								
	6	4			3			

Puzzle 433

		2			7	4		9
6							8	
8	3		9					2
	2	5		9				
				5		9	1	
7					6		5	4
	4							3
5		6	3			7		

Puzzle 434

					1		2	
					7	5		
4			9	2			3	
		4		3				1
7			2		4			8
3				7		6		
	5			6	3			9
		6	1					
	4		8					

Answers on Page 298

Puzzle 435

		4	7				3	
		8					6	7
				3			5	4
			4	1				5
			5		7			
	1			9	3			
	3	1		4				
	6	2				8		
	5				9	2		

Puzzle 436

	3	5		8				
		6			7			2
	9				5	3		
	2						1	
			6		2			
	5						3	
		9	8				5	
4			7			9		
				1		6	8	

Puzzle 437

6	3				7			
			9				4	
9		1						
1		8		6	2	9		
	6						2	
		4	8	3		5		6
						8		5
	7				9			
			3				6	7

Puzzle 438

4			6			2		
7		1		2	5			
5			7			6		9
2			4		6			7
9		6			3			1
			2	4		1		6
		5			8			3

Answers on Page 298

4				9		6		
				7	4	3		8
	7	5			6			
						2	3	
1								6
	9	2						
			3			7	9	
9		1	8	2				
		6		4				5

		4			6		9	
			2		8	4		
1	5					7		
3							1	
	7		5		9		8	
	8							9
		7					4	5
		6	8		5			
	4		9			3		

Puzzle 441

		3		8	4			
								4
	8	4				2		1
2			5		7	1		
				3				
		9	6		8			2
6		1				3	7	
5								
			9	7		5		

Puzzle 442

8		1	7			4		
6					4		3	
							2	1
	4			8				
2	8						9	4
				5			6	
7	1							
	2		9					6
		4			8	9		3

Answers on Page 298

Puzzle 443

			1		7			4
			8		6			3
				2		6		
5		9					4	
	8	2				5	7	
	6					1		9
		7		5				
6			9		3			
3			2		1			

Puzzle 444

	4							
5				7	2	3	4	
		8				7		2
	5		7	9				
		4				8		
				6	1		5	
2		6				1		
	9	7	2	8				6
							8	

Puzzle 445

9								7
			4				2	
	7	4	2	9			8	
	5		6					
4				8				9
					4		5	
	8			1	2	6	3	
	6				3			
7								5

Puzzle 446

1			6				9	
3		7	1					
	2		4					7
		3					7	6
4								2
6	8					5		
7					4		6	
					3	9		4
	9				1			8

Answers on Page 299

		8			4			3
		2	1		9			
	6			7			9	
	8			9			4	
4								7
	1			3			6	
	4			8			7	
			3		1	4		
6			5			3		

5	2						3	
		1			6			
			8			9		
	9			4	8			
1	8						2	6
			6	7			1	
		3			4			
			3			1		
	6						7	3

Puzzle 449

						6		
		3		4	8			
			7		2		8	3
	5					1		
	9	8	1		4	7	5	
		6					4	
1	4		2		7			
			5	6		4		
		2						

Puzzle 450

					7	6		
2	3		9					
8				2	3	1		
	7	5						
	2			4			7	
						8	5	
		3	2	5				9
					1		6	3
		9	7					

Answers on Page 299

	8							1
		9			6	5		
			9	5			2	
8	6				5			
2				3				8
			8				3	7
	1			4	3			
		4	5			3		
9							1	

	2		3					
1				2				
		3	1		4			5
	5				2			4
3		2				9		7
9			5				3	
8			2		5	1		
				8				9
				6			7	

Puzzle 453

			7					
						2		1
	9		6		8	3	7	
8		5						7
			3		5			
4						8		9
	6	7	2		1		9	
3		4						
					7			

Puzzle 454

9		8					7	
				6		8		1
	6				2		3	
	7			1	6	9		
		2	8	7			4	
	9		2				8	
7		1		3				
	2					4		5

Answers on Page 299

			4				3	5
		7						4
	9	4	2					
			6	7			1	
7								8
	1			4	9			
					8	1	2	
2						7		
6	7				3			

		2	1					8
			8	9	6			
				7				9
1		9				4	8	
	7						6	
	6	4				5		1
4				5				
			3	8	7			
8					9	1		

Puzzle 457

			5					
		5	7			1	8	
	4			1	8			
7	8							
6			2		7			1
							5	9
			8	4			2	
	1	8			3	9		
				2				

Puzzle 458

	7		9		8	6		
			6	5		1		
							4	
2	5			6				1
4								8
9				3			5	4
	2							
		3		9	6			
		6	5		1		8	

Answers on Page 300

6						2		
		8	2	3				
9		5	4				1	
3							4	
1			8		4			6
	4							9
	6				5	4		1
				2	6	7		
		1						5

		3						1
			8	5				
			4		1	9	2	
		6		2	5			4
1								7
3			1	9		8		
	6	7	5		4			
				6	2			
9						4		

Puzzle 461

9			1					
2	3							
		7		4			2	
		2			8			7
	6	5				3	9	
1			3			8		
	5			7		2		
							3	8
					6			1

Puzzle 462

3		4						
					7			8
	1			8		2		
7			2	3		4		6
			7		1			
8		2		9	5			1
		3		7			5	
9			6					
						3		7

Answers on Page 300

					7			
			5		2	8		
6	2	3	9					
7		1				3	2	
	6						9	
	8	2				1		4
					9	4	1	5
		5	7		1			
			2					

4	7					3		
	9			8			5	
1		2	4					
			3		9	8		
				2				
		1	8		6			
					2	7		6
	1			7			4	
		5					9	1

Puzzle 465

					1	9		
				3	8		1	
	4		9			7	2	
5	1					4		
		4				2		
		3					5	9
	6	2			5		9	
	8		7	9				
		5	8					

Puzzle 466

		8	1					
		5	8			7		3
	3			4				6
	6	2	7					1
4					5	6	7	
5				8			9	
1		9			4	5		
					7	1		

Answers on Page 300

Puzzle 467

			1	8		6		
					5			
9					3	8	2	
	6				1	4		
		2	3		4	1		
		7	9				5	
	8	6	2					3
			4					
		4		3	8			

Puzzle 468

			5					4
4					2			
				4	7			
	7				5	1		6
1	8			9			3	5
5		3	2				8	
		1	3					
			6					2
6				1				

Puzzle 469

	7		8	4		3		
	5							
9		3		7		1		
			5					6
		2	6		4	9		
	3				7			
		6		5		2		4
							1	
		7		3	1		8	

Puzzle 470

		1				9		7
8	7		4					
	3				7		4	
7	8			4	9			
			1	6			7	2
	9		2				8	
					8		9	3
1		8				2		

Puzzle 471

	8				4			
				1			4	
			6	8	1			5
	6	3					5	2
1								3
2	5					8	6	
9		5	8	2				
	3			4				
			3				9	

Puzzle 472

8						1	2	
		4			1			6
			5	8		9		
	1		6		5			
			7		8			
			4		9		5	
		1		7	2			
3			1			8		
	6	7						4

Puzzle 473

		2		7			1	9
	7	5		2		4		
9			7	3			8	
		7				6		
	8			9	5			3
		1		4		8	7	
2	9			6		1		

Puzzle 474

7			9		5	2		
			8	6			1	
				7		8		
						4	7	
2		5				1		8
	4	6						
		3		9				
	8			1	6			
		9	2		8			1

Answers on Page 301

Puzzle 475

5					6		9	
				1		7		
9					5	1		
3	4					9		
	6	5				8	4	
		8					6	3
		6	2					8
		7		3				
	5		6					7

Puzzle 476

		4		2	7			6
			6			9		
3					4	7		
						6	3	
		1		7		8		
	4	5						
		8	7					1
		2			6			
7			9	8		4		

Puzzle 477

8	6				9			
				5		4		
9	3		4		7			
6		9						
1	7						4	5
						8		6
		5		6		8	3
		6		7				
			1				9	7

Puzzle 478

				8	9			
					7	1	3	8
3						6	7	
			8	5				6
	3							9
6				3	1			
	9	6						4
4	7	5	6					
			4	2				

Answers on Page 301

6					4	1	3	
7								
	9		7	1	3			
9	8			6		4		
		6		3			2	9
			5	7	9		1	
								2
	1	5	2					4

8		2		7		4	3	
6			4					8
		6			8		1	
	9		7		1		4	
	7		3			6		
1					9			3
	3	9		1		2		4

Puzzle 481

		6		8		5	4	
			2			3		6
						8		
				6	8		1	
7			4		2			8
	2		1	5				
	4							
3		1			4			
	8	2		1		9		

Puzzle 482

6			3			2		
	3	2	7					9
				4			6	
			8			5	7	
			1		3			
	9	1			7			
	6			7				
1					5	9	4	
		8			4			5

Answers on Page 302

Puzzle 483

7				6		8	9	
	9				7			3
				3		5		
	4		3					1
	5						2	
6					1		5	
		3		1				
4			8				7	
	1	9		2				8

Puzzle 484

				1		9	4	
	7		3					6
		8			5			
						4		5
	9	3		7		2	6	
8		2						
			6			1		
7					8		9	
	2	1		3				

Puzzle 485

	3			7	5			8
				8		2		
					4		5	9
	1					5	7	
		7				4		
	6	4					2	
1	7		3					
		8		6				
5			7	4			6	

Puzzle 486

				1	9	7	6	
			2					
						8		3
		1		7	8	5	2	
				3				
	7	4	6	2		1		
8		5						
					7			
	1	2	8	6				

Answers on Page 302

Puzzle 487

6			4					7
		2	9	8		4		
				5		3	2	
								6
	1	4				8	5	
8								
	4	3		1				
		8		3	4	7		
9					2			3

Puzzle 488

7		8		6		1		2
		6		4		8		3
	2		8					
		9	5		6	2		
					7		1	
9		1		8		5		
4		5		2		6		8

Puzzle 489

7					6		2	3
				2	8	6		
9								
	7			1				
3			4		2			9
				9			3	
								6
		8	7	6				
4	9		2					1

Puzzle 490

	4	9				5	6	
					5	3		
		7						
	9		2					1
	8	2		9		4	5	
7					1		3	
						8		
		5	3					
	6	1				7	2	

Answers on Page 302

Puzzle 491

	4					7		
		9	6				4	1
1					7			8
4	7				3			
		8				9		
			8				5	7
9			1					6
5	6				2	4		
		7					1	

Puzzle 492

				5				
						5		3
		2	6	4	7		1	
	5					1		
3		9	1		5	8		6
		8					3	
	2		4	1	9	3		
7		1						
				2				

Puzzle 493

	9							
				7	3	1		4
	4				8		6	
3	2					8		
		4	2		5	6		
		6					1	7
	3		1				9	
8		5	3	9				
							7	

Puzzle 494

			6	2	4	8	1	
		1				3	7	
3	7				8	6		
				7				
		5	4				2	7
	1	3				2		
	8	4	5	1	9			

Answers on Page 303

3	1			9				4
	6				4			3
		2	5			8		
	5			6				
			4		7			
				8			3	
		7			2	5		
1			3				7	
8				7			2	1

				5			8	
6	8							9
		1	9		7		6	
	3			1		9		
9								5
		2		6			7	
	7		2		5	8		
2							5	4
	9			3				

Puzzle 497

9			7	6	1		4	
7				9	4	6		
8	6					5	7	
	2	4					3	6
		3	5	8				2
	4		3	1	7			9

Puzzle 498

		1				7	4	3
		9		2	7			
			5	1				
			6		1	3		
	9						1	
		4	2		8			
				7	9			
			8	3		5		
2	8	3				9		

Answers on Page 303

```
. 6 . | 3 . . | 2 . .
. . . | . . . | . . 3
3 2 8 | . 5 . | . . 1
------+-------+------
. . 6 | 5 . 9 | . . .
. 1 . | . . . | . 8 .
. . . | 6 . 7 | 4 . .
------+-------+------
1 . . | . 2 . | 9 7 6
2 . . | . . . | . . .
. . 9 | . . 3 | . 5 .
```

```
7 . . | 2 . . | 5 . .
1 . . | . . 6 | . . .
. . . | . 9 3 | . . 6
------+-------+------
6 . . | . . . | 1 9 .
. 4 8 | . . . | 7 2 .
. 1 2 | . . . | . . 4
------+-------+------
8 . . | 4 5 . | . . .
. . . | 3 . . | . . 1
. . 6 | . . 2 | . . 9
```

Puzzle 501

	7	5					3	
	1				9			7
				7		6		5
		6	8					
3			4		5			1
				3	4			
8		4		9				
9			7				2	
	2					1	8	

Puzzle 502

		1		7	5		6	
							2	1
	6							3
2	3				4			
6				9				7
			8				3	9
5							4	
1	9							
	4		6	2		3		

Answers on Page 303

	8					6		
6				4	8		5	3
		9			6			
				3		4		
	5		1		9		3	
		1		2				
			3			2		
9	1		4	7				6
		7					9	

		2				1	4	
	5			4				
8			1		2			
		6		7			5	
		3		9		8		
	2			3		6		
			4		5			7
				2			1	
	6	7				9		

Puzzle 505

7								
		8		9		1	4	
	9		1			5		
			6				5	8
			4	1	2			
6	7				5			
		1			9		8	
	6	3		7		2		
								5

Puzzle 506

				6		5	4	9
					5			
		5	1					8
	1						7	4
	7		4		9		2	
2	5						8	
3					1	2		
			2					
6	2	7		8				

Answers on Page 304

8				6		4		
	4		2					
	7				3		8	
		6		4	7	2		
				2				
		2	6	5		8		
	3		5				1	
					2		5	
		5		1				9

				5				
	8	1			7	5		
			8	1			4	
							8	7
1			7		2			6
9	5							
	2			4	8			
		9	3			8	1	
				2				

Answers

PUZZLE 1

4	2	3	1
3	1	2	4
1	3	4	2
2	4	1	3

PUZZLE 2

3	2	1	4
1	4	3	2
2	3	4	1
4	1	2	3

PUZZLE 3

1	4	3	2
2	3	4	1
4	1	2	3
3	2	1	4

PUZZLE 4

2	3	4	1
4	1	3	2
1	4	2	3
3	2	1	4

PUZZLE 5

1	4	2	3
3	2	4	1
4	3	1	2
2	1	3	4

PUZZLE 6

3	4	2	1
2	1	4	3
4	3	1	2
1	2	3	4

PUZZLE 7

3	4	2	1
2	1	3	4
4	2	1	3
1	3	4	2

PUZZLE 8

4	3	1	2
2	1	4	3
1	2	3	4
3	4	2	1

PUZZLE 9

2	3	1	4
1	4	2	3
3	1	4	2
4	2	3	1

PUZZLE 10

1	2	3	4
3	4	2	1
4	3	1	2
2	1	4	3

PUZZLE 11

1	2	3	4
3	4	1	2
2	3	4	1
4	1	2	3

PUZZLE 12

1	3	4	2
2	4	3	1
4	2	1	3
3	1	2	4

PUZZLE 13

2	1	4	3
3	4	1	2
4	2	3	1
1	3	2	4

PUZZLE 14

2	3	1	4
4	1	3	2
1	2	4	3
3	4	2	1

PUZZLE 15

4	3	1	2
2	1	4	3
1	2	3	4
3	4	2	1

PUZZLE 16

1	4	2	3
3	2	4	1
4	1	3	2
2	3	1	4

PUZZLE 17

3	4	2	1
2	1	3	4
4	2	1	3
1	3	4	2

PUZZLE 18

3	2	4	1
1	4	2	3
2	1	3	4
4	3	1	2

PUZZLE 19

2	4	1	3
1	3	2	4
4	1	3	2
3	2	4	1

PUZZLE 20

4	3	2	1
2	1	4	3
1	4	3	2
3	2	1	4

PUZZLE 21

3	1	2	4
2	4	1	3
4	2	3	1
1	3	4	2

PUZZLE 22

4	2	1	3
1	3	2	4
3	1	4	2
2	4	3	1

PUZZLE 23

2	4	1	3
3	1	4	2
1	2	3	4
4	3	2	1

PUZZLE 24

1	2	3	4
3	4	1	2
4	1	2	3
2	3	4	1

Answers

2	3	1	4
4	1	3	2
1	4	2	3
3	2	4	1

PUZZLE 25

3	2	1	4
4	1	2	3
1	4	3	2
2	3	4	1

PUZZLE 26

4	2	3	1
3	1	4	2
1	4	2	3
2	3	1	4

PUZZLE 27

1	4	3	2
2	3	4	1
3	1	2	4
4	2	1	3

PUZZLE 28

1	2	3	4
4	3	2	1
3	4	1	2
2	1	4	3

PUZZLE 29

2	3	4	1
4	1	2	3
1	2	3	4
3	4	1	2

PUZZLE 30

4	3	2	1
1	2	3	4
3	1	4	2
2	4	1	3

PUZZLE 31

2	4	1	3
1	3	2	4
3	2	4	1
4	1	3	2

PUZZLE 32

3	4	1	2
1	2	3	4
4	1	2	3
2	3	4	1

PUZZLE 33

1	3	2	4
2	4	1	3
4	2	3	1
3	1	4	2

PUZZLE 34

2	1	3	4
3	4	2	1
4	2	1	3
1	3	4	2

PUZZLE 35

1	4	3	2
3	2	4	1
4	1	2	3
2	3	1	4

PUZZLE 36

PUZZLE 37

1	4	2	3
2	3	1	4
3	1	4	2
4	2	3	1

PUZZLE 38

1	2	4	3
4	3	1	2
2	4	3	1
3	1	2	4

PUZZLE 39

2	3	4	1
4	1	2	3
3	4	1	2
1	2	3	4

PUZZLE 40

1	4	2	3
2	3	1	4
3	2	4	1
4	1	3	2

PUZZLE 41

4	1	3	2
2	3	4	1
1	4	2	3
3	2	1	4

PUZZLE 42

1	2	3	4
4	3	2	1
2	1	4	3
3	4	1	2

PUZZLE 43

2	4	3	1
3	1	2	4
4	2	1	3
1	3	4	2

PUZZLE 44

1	3	2	4
2	4	3	1
4	2	1	3
3	1	4	2

PUZZLE 45

5	4	1	6	3	2
2	3	6	4	1	5
6	1	5	2	4	3
3	2	4	1	5	6
1	6	3	5	2	4
4	5	2	3	6	1

PUZZLE 46

3	2	1	6	5	4
5	6	4	1	3	2
4	3	6	2	1	5
1	5	2	4	6	3
6	4	3	5	2	1
2	1	5	3	4	6

PUZZLE 47

2	6	3	4	1	5
1	4	5	3	2	6
3	1	2	5	6	4
6	5	4	2	3	1
5	2	6	1	4	3
4	3	1	6	5	2

PUZZLE 48

5	4	2	3	1	6
6	3	1	4	5	2
4	1	3	2	6	5
2	5	6	1	3	4
1	6	4	5	2	3
3	2	5	6	4	1

Answers

PUZZLE 49

5	1	4	3	2	6
6	2	3	1	4	5
4	6	5	2	3	1
1	3	2	6	5	4
2	5	1	4	6	3
3	4	6	5	1	2

PUZZLE 50

1	6	5	4	3	2
2	3	4	6	1	5
6	5	2	1	4	3
4	1	3	2	5	6
3	2	1	5	6	4
5	4	6	3	2	1

PUZZLE 51

2	3	1	4	5	6
4	5	6	1	2	3
3	1	4	5	6	2
5	6	2	3	4	1
1	2	5	6	3	4
6	4	3	2	1	5

PUZZLE 52

5	6	4	2	1	3
1	2	3	5	6	4
4	5	6	3	2	1
2	3	1	6	4	5
6	1	5	4	3	2
3	4	2	1	5	6

PUZZLE 53

4	1	6	2	5	3
2	5	3	6	4	1
6	3	5	1	2	4
1	4	2	3	6	5
3	6	4	5	1	2
5	2	1	4	3	6

PUZZLE 54

3	2	4	5	1	6
6	1	5	2	3	4
5	6	1	3	4	2
4	3	2	6	5	1
2	4	3	1	6	5
1	5	6	4	2	3

PUZZLE 55

4	1	5	3	6	2
2	3	6	4	1	5
3	4	2	1	5	6
5	6	1	2	3	4
6	2	3	5	4	1
1	5	4	6	2	3

PUZZLE 56

4	3	6	2	5	1
1	2	5	6	4	3
5	4	2	3	1	6
6	1	3	5	2	4
3	5	4	1	6	2
2	6	1	4	3	5

PUZZLE 57

6	3	4	2	5	1
2	5	1	6	3	4
4	1	6	5	2	3
5	2	3	4	1	6
3	6	5	1	4	2
1	4	2	3	6	5

PUZZLE 58

3	4	6	2	5	1
1	2	5	4	3	6
2	1	3	5	6	4
5	6	4	3	1	2
4	3	1	6	2	5
6	5	2	1	4	3

PUZZLE 59

1	4	6	3	2	5
5	2	3	6	1	4
4	5	1	2	3	6
6	3	2	4	5	1
3	1	4	5	6	2
2	6	5	1	4	3

PUZZLE 60

5	2	1	3	4	6
6	4	3	5	2	1
1	5	6	4	3	2
2	3	4	1	6	5
3	6	5	2	1	4
4	1	2	6	5	3

1	6	4	5	2	3
2	3	5	1	4	6
6	2	3	4	5	1
5	4	1	3	6	2
3	5	2	6	1	4
4	1	6	2	3	5

PUZZLE 61

4	2	3	5	6	1
5	1	6	3	2	4
2	4	5	1	3	6
6	3	1	2	4	5
1	6	2	4	5	3
3	5	4	6	1	2

PUZZLE 62

4	5	1	6	3	2
3	6	2	5	4	1
6	2	4	3	1	5
5	1	3	2	6	4
1	3	5	4	2	6
2	4	6	1	5	3

PUZZLE 63

2	5	1	4	6	3
4	6	3	5	2	1
6	2	5	3	1	4
3	1	4	2	5	6
5	4	6	1	3	2
1	3	2	6	4	5

PUZZLE 64

3	4	2	1	5	6
1	6	5	2	4	3
5	3	6	4	2	1
2	1	4	6	3	5
6	2	3	5	1	4
4	5	1	3	6	2

PUZZLE 65

1	6	4	3	2	5
5	2	3	4	6	1
2	3	1	5	4	6
4	5	6	1	3	2
6	4	5	2	1	3
3	1	2	6	5	4

PUZZLE 66

5	4	6	3	2	1
1	2	3	4	6	5
4	3	2	5	1	6
6	1	5	2	3	4
2	6	4	1	5	3
3	5	1	6	4	2

PUZZLE 67

3	2	5	1	4	6
1	4	6	5	2	3
4	3	1	6	5	2
5	6	2	3	1	4
6	1	4	2	3	5
2	5	3	4	6	1

PUZZLE 68

6	2	1	5	4	3
3	4	5	2	1	6
5	1	3	4	6	2
2	6	4	3	5	1
4	3	6	1	2	5
1	5	2	6	3	4

PUZZLE 69

4	1	2	6	3	5
3	6	5	2	1	4
5	4	3	1	2	6
1	2	6	5	4	3
6	3	1	4	5	2
2	5	4	3	6	1

PUZZLE 70

4	2	6	1	3	5
5	3	1	6	2	4
1	4	2	3	5	6
6	5	3	2	4	1
3	1	4	5	6	2
2	6	5	4	1	3

PUZZLE 71

4	5	2	1	3	6
3	1	6	2	4	5
1	6	3	5	2	4
2	4	5	3	6	1
5	3	4	6	1	2
6	2	1	4	5	3

PUZZLE 72

PUZZLE 73

2	6	5	3	4	1
4	1	3	6	2	5
1	3	4	5	6	2
6	5	2	1	3	4
5	4	6	2	1	3
3	2	1	4	5	6

PUZZLE 74

1	3	2	4	5	6
4	6	5	1	3	2
2	1	6	3	4	5
5	4	3	6	2	1
3	2	1	5	6	4
6	5	4	2	1	3

PUZZLE 75

6	5	1	4	3	2
3	4	2	5	1	6
4	1	6	2	5	3
2	3	5	1	6	4
5	2	3	6	4	1
1	6	4	3	2	5

PUZZLE 76

3	5	1	6	2	4
6	4	2	5	3	1
4	1	5	3	6	2
2	6	3	1	4	5
5	2	6	4	1	3
1	3	4	2	5	6

PUZZLE 77

6	2	5	4	3	1
1	3	4	6	2	5
3	5	1	2	4	6
2	4	6	1	5	3
5	6	2	3	1	4
4	1	3	5	6	2

PUZZLE 78

4	3	2	5	6	1
1	5	6	3	2	4
2	1	5	6	4	3
6	4	3	2	1	5
3	2	1	4	5	6
5	6	4	1	3	2

PUZZLE 79

4	6	5	2	1	3
1	2	3	5	4	6
3	4	2	6	5	1
6	5	1	4	3	2
5	1	6	3	2	4
2	3	4	1	6	5

PUZZLE 80

4	3	5	6	1	2
6	2	1	4	5	3
5	4	6	3	2	1
2	1	3	5	6	4
1	5	4	2	3	6
3	6	2	1	4	5

PUZZLE 81

6	3	4	2	5	1
2	1	5	3	6	4
3	2	6	1	4	5
5	4	1	6	3	2
4	6	2	5	1	3
1	5	3	4	2	6

PUZZLE 82

6	4	3	1	2	5
2	5	1	4	6	3
5	1	6	2	3	4
4	3	2	6	5	1
3	6	4	5	1	2
1	2	5	3	4	6

PUZZLE 83

6	5	4	2	3	1
3	1	2	5	6	4
4	6	1	3	2	5
5	2	3	4	1	6
2	4	6	1	5	3
1	3	5	6	4	2

PUZZLE 84

6	2	4	1	5	3
5	3	1	6	4	2
3	1	6	5	2	4
4	5	2	3	6	1
2	6	3	4	1	5
1	4	5	2	3	6

PUZZLE 85

6	1	4	3	2	5
2	5	3	4	1	6
3	2	6	5	4	1
5	4	1	2	6	3
1	3	2	6	5	4
4	6	5	1	3	2

PUZZLE 86

4	3	1	5	2	6
6	5	2	1	4	3
5	4	6	2	3	1
1	2	3	6	5	4
3	6	5	4	1	2
2	1	4	3	6	5

PUZZLE 87

6	3	4	5	2	1
1	5	2	6	3	4
2	1	5	3	4	6
4	6	3	2	1	5
5	2	1	4	6	3
3	4	6	1	5	2

PUZZLE 88

5	3	2	4	6	1
6	1	4	3	5	2
4	6	5	1	2	3
1	2	3	5	4	6
2	5	1	6	3	4
3	4	6	2	1	5

PUZZLE 89

5	2	1	4	3	6
3	4	6	2	1	5
4	6	5	1	2	3
1	3	2	5	6	4
2	5	3	6	4	1
6	1	4	3	5	2

PUZZLE 90

5	2	6	3	1	4
3	1	4	2	6	5
4	5	2	6	3	1
1	6	3	4	5	2
6	4	1	5	2	3
2	3	5	1	4	6

PUZZLE 91

2	4	5	1	6	3
1	6	3	4	5	2
5	2	1	3	4	6
6	3	4	5	2	1
4	1	6	2	3	5
3	5	2	6	1	4

PUZZLE 92

3	6	2	4	1	5
5	4	1	2	3	6
6	1	5	3	4	2
2	3	4	5	6	1
4	5	6	1	2	3
1	2	3	6	5	4

PUZZLE 93

5	6	4	2	3	1
1	2	3	5	4	6
2	5	6	3	1	4
4	3	1	6	2	5
6	4	2	1	5	3
3	1	5	4	6	2

PUZZLE 94

3	4	6	1	5	2
5	2	1	3	4	6
1	5	4	6	2	3
2	6	3	4	1	5
6	1	5	2	3	4
4	3	2	5	6	1

PUZZLE 95

3	6	1	2	4	5
4	5	2	6	3	1
5	4	6	3	1	2
2	1	3	5	6	4
1	3	5	4	2	6
6	2	4	1	5	3

PUZZLE 96

2	1	4	5	6	3
5	6	3	1	2	4
3	4	6	2	1	5
1	5	2	3	4	6
4	2	5	6	3	1
6	3	1	4	5	2

PUZZLE 97

2	3	6	1	5	4
4	1	5	2	3	6
6	2	3	4	1	5
5	4	1	6	2	3
3	6	2	5	4	1
1	5	4	3	6	2

PUZZLE 98

4	5	3	2	1	6
1	6	2	4	5	3
3	1	4	5	6	2
6	2	5	3	4	1
2	4	6	1	3	5
5	3	1	6	2	4

PUZZLE 99

3	2	5	6	1	4
4	6	1	5	3	2
2	1	4	3	6	5
5	3	6	4	2	1
1	4	3	2	5	6
6	5	2	1	4	3

PUZZLE 100

5	6	2	3	4	1
1	4	3	5	6	2
6	2	1	4	3	5
3	5	4	2	1	6
4	1	5	6	2	3
2	3	6	1	5	4

PUZZLE 101

4	5	2	1	6	3
6	3	1	4	5	2
2	6	3	5	1	4
5	1	4	3	2	6
3	2	5	6	4	1
1	4	6	2	3	5

PUZZLE 102

4	5	3	1	6	2
6	2	1	4	5	3
3	4	5	2	1	6
1	6	2	3	4	5
5	3	4	6	2	1
2	1	6	5	3	4

PUZZLE 103

6	2	5	1	3	4
1	3	4	2	5	6
4	1	3	6	2	5
5	6	2	4	1	3
2	5	6	3	4	1
3	4	1	5	6	2

PUZZLE 104

1	6	3	4	2	5
4	2	5	6	3	1
2	3	1	5	4	6
5	4	6	3	1	2
6	1	4	2	5	3
3	5	2	1	6	4

PUZZLE 105

4	5	6	2	3	1
3	1	2	6	5	4
2	3	4	1	6	5
1	6	5	3	4	2
5	2	3	4	1	6
6	4	1	5	2	3

PUZZLE 106

6	1	3	5	4	2
2	5	4	6	1	3
4	2	5	3	6	1
3	6	1	2	5	4
1	3	6	4	2	5
5	4	2	1	3	6

PUZZLE 107

2	6	4	3	1	5
5	3	1	4	2	6
6	4	2	1	5	3
3	1	5	2	6	4
1	5	3	6	4	2
4	2	6	5	3	1

PUZZLE 108

6	2	3	4	1	5
4	1	5	2	3	6
5	3	4	6	2	1
1	6	2	3	5	4
3	4	1	5	6	2
2	5	6	1	4	3

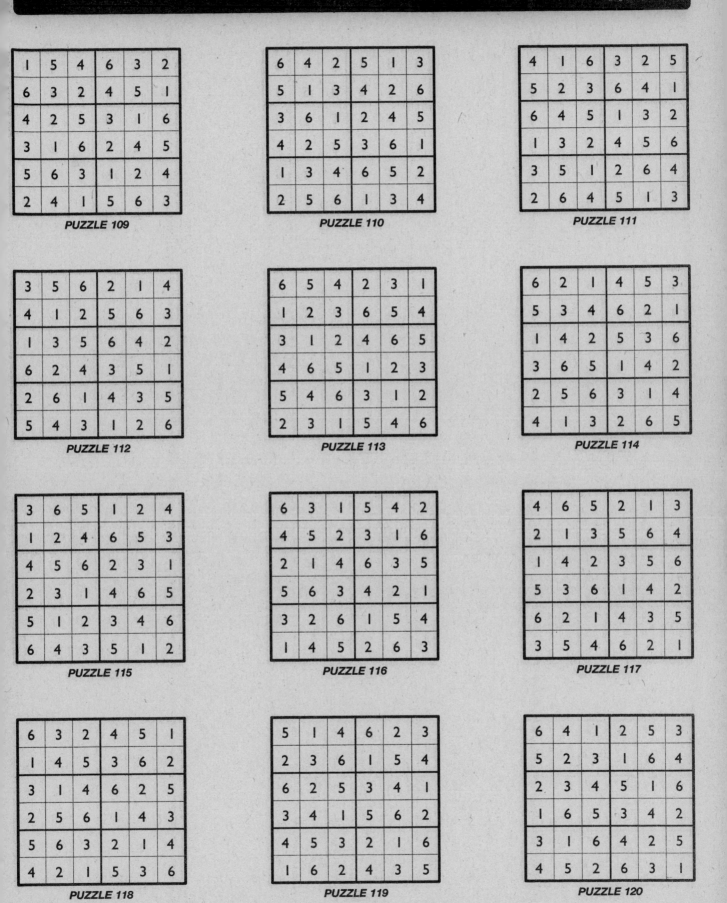

PUZZLE 109

1	5	4	6	3	2
6	3	2	4	5	1
4	2	5	3	1	6
3	1	6	2	4	5
5	6	3	1	2	4
2	4	1	5	6	3

PUZZLE 110

6	4	2	5	1	3
5	1	3	4	2	6
3	6	1	2	4	5
4	2	5	3	6	1
1	3	4	6	5	2
2	5	6	1	3	4

PUZZLE 111

4	1	6	3	2	5
5	2	3	6	4	1
6	4	5	1	3	2
1	3	2	4	5	6
3	5	1	2	6	4
2	6	4	5	1	3

PUZZLE 112

3	5	6	2	1	4
4	1	2	5	6	3
1	3	5	6	4	2
6	2	4	3	5	1
2	6	1	4	3	5
5	4	3	1	2	6

PUZZLE 113

6	5	4	2	3	1
1	2	3	6	5	4
3	1	2	4	6	5
4	6	5	1	2	3
5	4	6	3	1	2
2	3	1	5	4	6

PUZZLE 114

6	2	1	4	5	3
5	3	4	6	2	1
1	4	2	5	3	6
3	6	5	1	4	2
2	5	6	3	1	4
4	1	3	2	6	5

PUZZLE 115

3	6	5	1	2	4
1	2	4	6	5	3
4	5	6	2	3	1
2	3	1	4	6	5
5	1	2	3	4	6
6	4	3	5	1	2

PUZZLE 116

6	3	1	5	4	2
4	5	2	3	1	6
2	1	4	6	3	5
5	6	3	4	2	1
3	2	6	1	5	4
1	4	5	2	6	3

PUZZLE 117

4	6	5	2	1	3
2	1	3	5	6	4
1	4	2	3	5	6
5	3	6	1	4	2
6	2	1	4	3	5
3	5	4	6	2	1

PUZZLE 118

6	3	2	4	5	1
1	4	5	3	6	2
3	1	4	6	2	5
2	5	6	1	4	3
5	6	3	2	1	4
4	2	1	5	3	6

PUZZLE 119

5	1	4	6	2	3
2	3	6	1	5	4
6	2	5	3	4	1
3	4	1	5	6	2
4	5	3	2	1	6
1	6	2	4	3	5

PUZZLE 120

6	4	1	2	5	3
5	2	3	1	6	4
2	3	4	5	1	6
1	6	5	3	4	2
3	1	6	4	2	5
4	5	2	6	3	1

Answers

PUZZLE 121

2	3	6	1	5	4
1	5	4	3	6	2
4	2	3	6	1	5
5	6	1	4	2	3
3	1	5	2	4	6
6	4	2	5	3	1

PUZZLE 122

3	1	6	5	4	2
2	5	4	3	1	6
1	6	5	4	2	3
4	2	3	6	5	1
6	4	2	1	3	5
5	3	1	2	6	4

PUZZLE 123

4	6	2	1	3	5
5	1	3	2	4	6
1	3	5	4	6	2
6	2	4	3	5	1
2	4	6	5	1	3
3	5	1	6	2	4

PUZZLE 124

3	6	2	5	1	4
4	5	1	3	6	2
6	2	3	1	4	5
5	1	4	6	2	3
1	4	5	2	3	6
2	3	6	4	5	1

PUZZLE 125

7	8	5	6	2	3	1	9	4
6	2	3	1	9	4	7	8	5
1	4	9	5	7	8	6	2	3
3	9	7	8	1	5	4	6	2
4	1	2	7	6	9	5	3	8
5	6	8	3	4	2	9	1	7
8	7	4	9	3	6	2	5	1
2	5	6	4	8	1	3	7	9
9	3	1	2	5	7	8	4	6

PUZZLE 126

1	9	8	7	5	4	6	3	2
5	7	3	1	2	6	8	9	4
4	2	6	9	3	8	7	1	5
9	8	1	5	6	3	4	2	7
3	5	4	2	8	7	1	6	9
2	6	7	4	9	1	3	5	8
8	1	9	3	4	2	5	7	6
7	4	2	6	1	5	9	8	3
6	3	5	8	7	9	2	4	1

PUZZLE 127

4	8	5	2	6	7	1	3	9
9	1	6	3	8	4	7	2	5
3	7	2	1	9	5	8	6	4
6	2	7	9	3	1	4	5	8
8	9	3	4	5	6	2	7	1
1	5	4	7	2	8	3	9	6
7	6	8	5	1	3	9	4	2
5	3	9	8	4	2	6	1	7
2	4	1	6	7	9	5	8	3

PUZZLE 128

9	7	2	5	4	1	8	6	3
1	6	5	3	8	9	7	2	4
8	4	3	6	2	7	1	9	5
5	1	6	4	7	8	2	3	9
3	2	4	1	9	5	6	7	8
7	9	8	2	3	6	4	5	1
4	3	9	8	6	2	5	1	7
2	8	1	7	5	3	9	4	6
6	5	7	9	1	4	3	8	2

PUZZLE 129

7	6	3	1	9	4	2	5	8
8	4	2	5	3	7	1	6	9
1	5	9	2	8	6	3	7	4
6	1	7	8	4	5	9	2	3
3	2	5	6	1	9	8	4	7
9	8	4	7	2	3	5	1	6
5	3	1	4	6	8	7	9	2
4	7	8	9	5	2	6	3	1
2	9	6	3	7	1	4	8	5

PUZZLE 130

2	1	9	4	5	8	7	3	6
5	6	4	3	7	1	8	2	9
8	7	3	9	6	2	1	5	4
1	8	6	2	9	5	4	7	3
4	9	5	1	3	7	2	6	8
7	3	2	8	4	6	5	9	1
3	5	7	6	1	4	9	8	2
9	2	1	5	8	3	6	4	7
6	4	8	7	2	9	3	1	5

PUZZLE 131

2	5	1	7	3	6	9	4	8
8	9	3	1	2	4	5	6	7
6	4	7	8	5	9	3	1	2
5	6	9	3	8	1	7	2	4
3	8	2	6	4	7	1	5	9
7	1	4	2	9	5	6	8	3
4	7	6	9	1	2	8	3	5
9	2	8	5	6	3	4	7	1
1	3	5	4	7	8	2	9	6

PUZZLE 132

1	2	4	6	9	7	3	5	8
3	6	7	4	8	5	2	1	9
5	9	8	3	2	1	6	7	4
7	3	1	9	4	8	5	2	6
6	4	2	1	5	3	9	8	7
8	5	9	2	7	6	1	4	3
9	1	5	8	3	4	7	6	2
2	8	6	7	1	9	4	3	5
4	7	3	5	6	2	8	9	1

PUZZLE 133

8	3	5	2	7	9	4	1	6
9	6	4	1	8	3	7	2	5
1	7	2	6	5	4	8	3	9
2	4	8	3	1	5	9	6	7
6	9	1	7	2	8	5	4	3
3	5	7	9	4	6	2	8	1
7	1	3	4	9	2	6	5	8
5	2	9	8	6	1	3	7	4
4	8	6	5	3	7	1	9	2

PUZZLE 134

8	9	1	4	2	3	6	7	5
4	6	5	9	8	7	1	2	3
2	3	7	5	1	6	9	8	4
7	8	6	2	5	1	3	4	9
3	5	4	6	7	9	8	1	2
9	1	2	8	3	4	7	5	6
6	2	9	7	4	8	5	3	1
5	7	3	1	6	2	4	9	8
1	4	8	3	9	5	2	6	7

PUZZLE 135

5	2	6	7	8	3	9	1	4
4	8	1	9	6	5	3	2	7
3	9	7	2	4	1	5	6	8
2	3	4	1	7	8	6	5	9
6	7	5	4	3	9	1	8	2
9	1	8	5	2	6	4	7	3
1	4	2	3	5	7	8	9	6
8	5	3	6	9	2	7	4	1
7	6	9	8	1	4	2	3	5

PUZZLE 136

8	7	2	4	6	1	5	3	9
1	3	5	9	7	8	2	4	6
6	4	9	3	2	5	7	1	8
3	8	6	5	1	2	4	9	7
5	1	4	7	3	9	8	6	2
9	2	7	6	8	4	3	5	1
7	5	3	2	9	6	1	8	4
2	6	1	8	4	3	9	7	5
4	9	8	1	5	7	6	2	3

PUZZLE 137

7	4	2	3	8	1	5	6	9
9	1	6	4	2	5	7	3	8
3	8	5	6	7	9	2	4	1
8	2	1	9	4	7	3	5	6
5	3	4	2	1	6	8	9	7
6	9	7	5	3	8	1	2	4
4	6	8	1	5	2	9	7	3
1	5	9	7	6	3	4	8	2
2	7	3	8	9	4	6	1	5

PUZZLE 138

6	4	3	7	5	2	9	1	8
9	1	8	6	4	3	5	2	7
2	7	5	8	1	9	6	4	3
4	5	9	1	3	8	7	6	2
7	3	1	4	2	6	8	9	5
8	6	2	9	7	5	1	3	4
5	8	4	3	9	1	2	7	6
3	9	6	2	8	7	4	5	1
1	2	7	5	6	4	3	8	9

PUZZLE 139

4	6	7	8	1	5	2	3	9
8	2	9	7	4	3	1	6	5
1	3	5	2	9	6	7	4	8
6	8	1	9	5	2	4	7	3
5	7	2	4	3	8	9	1	6
3	9	4	1	6	7	8	5	2
2	1	6	5	7	9	3	8	4
9	4	3	6	8	1	5	2	7
7	5	8	3	2	4	6	9	1

PUZZLE 140

8	4	6	1	2	5	7	3	9
9	1	7	6	3	4	5	2	8
2	3	5	7	9	8	6	4	1
7	9	4	8	5	2	1	6	3
6	8	1	3	4	7	9	5	2
5	2	3	9	6	1	8	7	4
1	5	2	4	7	9	3	8	6
3	7	9	2	8	6	4	1	5
4	6	8	5	1	3	2	9	7

PUZZLE 141

5	7	8	4	2	3	1	6	9
2	4	1	9	6	8	3	7	5
3	9	6	7	1	5	2	4	8
1	8	9	5	7	6	4	2	3
4	6	2	3	8	1	9	5	7
7	3	5	2	4	9	6	8	1
6	1	3	8	5	2	7	9	4
9	5	7	6	3	4	8	1	2
8	2	4	1	9	7	5	3	6

PUZZLE 142

6	1	2	8	3	9	7	5	4
9	8	5	4	2	7	6	1	3
4	7	3	5	1	6	9	2	8
1	3	6	2	4	8	5	9	7
8	5	9	6	7	3	2	4	1
7	2	4	9	5	1	8	3	6
2	4	7	3	8	5	1	6	9
3	6	1	7	9	2	4	8	5
5	9	8	1	6	4	3	7	2

PUZZLE 143

2	7	9	8	3	5	6	4	1
3	8	1	7	6	4	9	2	5
4	5	6	9	1	2	7	8	3
7	1	4	2	8	3	5	9	6
8	6	3	4	5	9	1	7	2
5	9	2	1	7	6	4	3	8
1	2	5	3	4	7	8	6	9
6	3	7	5	9	8	2	1	4
9	4	8	6	2	1	3	5	7

PUZZLE 144

5	4	7	3	9	1	6	2	8
6	1	8	2	5	7	4	3	9
3	2	9	8	4	6	7	1	5
1	8	6	5	7	2	9	4	3
7	3	5	4	8	9	1	6	2
2	9	4	6	1	3	8	5	7
9	7	3	1	2	4	5	8	6
8	6	1	7	3	5	2	9	4
4	5	2	9	6	8	3	7	1

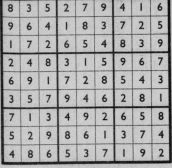

PUZZLE 145

5	3	2	7	9	1	4	6	8
9	1	6	2	8	4	5	3	7
7	8	4	6	5	3	2	1	9
1	7	9	3	4	8	6	2	5
4	2	3	5	7	6	9	8	1
6	5	8	1	2	9	7	4	3
2	6	1	9	3	7	8	5	4
8	9	5	4	1	2	3	7	6
3	4	7	8	6	5	1	9	2

PUZZLE 146

7	9	8	4	1	2	6	3	5
3	6	2	8	5	7	9	1	4
1	5	4	3	9	6	7	2	8
4	3	5	6	7	1	8	9	2
8	7	9	2	3	4	1	5	6
2	1	6	5	8	9	3	4	7
5	8	7	1	2	3	4	6	9
6	2	1	9	4	8	5	7	3
9	4	3	7	6	5	2	8	1

PUZZLE 147

1	5	3	2	7	4	9	6	8
7	4	8	9	6	1	2	3	5
6	2	9	8	3	5	4	7	1
8	3	5	7	9	2	1	4	6
2	7	1	6	4	3	5	8	9
4	9	6	1	5	8	7	2	3
5	6	7	4	8	9	3	1	2
9	1	4	3	2	6	8	5	7
3	8	2	5	1	7	6	9	4

PUZZLE 148

8	7	6	9	3	1	4	2	5
4	2	3	5	6	8	7	1	9
9	1	5	7	4	2	3	6	8
3	9	7	4	5	6	2	8	1
6	8	1	2	9	3	5	7	4
5	4	2	8	1	7	9	3	6
7	3	4	6	8	5	1	9	2
2	6	9	1	7	4	8	5	3
1	5	8	3	2	9	6	4	7

PUZZLE 149

3	4	6	9	8	5	1	2	7
9	1	8	6	7	2	3	5	4
2	5	7	1	4	3	6	9	8
5	7	9	3	6	8	2	4	1
8	3	2	4	1	7	5	6	9
1	6	4	2	5	9	7	8	3
7	8	3	5	2	4	9	1	6
6	9	5	8	3	1	4	7	2
4	2	1	7	9	6	8	3	5

PUZZLE 150

9	7	5	2	8	3	1	6	4
4	1	8	6	7	5	3	9	2
2	3	6	9	1	4	7	5	8
5	9	1	7	4	8	6	2	3
7	6	2	5	3	9	8	4	1
8	4	3	1	6	2	9	7	5
6	2	4	8	9	1	5	3	7
3	8	7	4	5	6	2	1	9
1	5	9	3	2	7	4	8	6

PUZZLE 151

6	7	8	2	9	5	3	1	4
9	5	3	7	1	4	2	8	6
1	4	2	3	8	6	9	5	7
4	9	7	5	3	2	1	6	8
2	3	1	6	7	8	4	9	5
5	8	6	1	4	9	7	2	3
3	1	9	8	6	7	5	4	2
8	2	4	9	5	3	6	7	1
7	6	5	4	2	1	8	3	9

PUZZLE 152

6	3	2	1	4	5	8	9	7
9	4	5	6	8	7	3	2	1
1	7	8	3	9	2	5	4	6
3	9	1	7	6	4	2	5	8
5	8	7	9	2	1	4	6	3
4	2	6	5	3	8	7	1	9
8	6	4	2	1	3	9	7	5
7	1	3	4	5	9	6	8	2
2	5	9	8	7	6	1	3	4

PUZZLE 153

4	2	8	9	1	3	6	7	5
1	5	9	7	2	6	4	8	3
6	7	3	8	5	4	1	9	2
2	4	5	3	6	8	7	1	9
7	3	6	4	9	1	2	5	8
9	8	1	2	7	5	3	4	6
8	6	4	1	3	9	5	2	7
5	1	7	6	8	2	9	3	4
3	9	2	5	4	7	8	6	1

PUZZLE 154

4	7	2	3	5	1	8	6	9
9	5	6	2	4	8	7	3	1
1	3	8	9	7	6	2	5	4
6	8	7	5	1	2	9	4	3
5	4	3	6	8	9	1	2	7
2	1	9	4	3	7	5	8	6
8	6	5	7	9	4	3	1	2
3	9	4	1	2	5	6	7	8
7	2	1	8	6	3	4	9	5

PUZZLE 155

9	6	3	4	2	1	8	7	5
8	1	5	3	7	6	9	4	2
7	4	2	8	5	9	6	3	1
6	9	7	5	4	2	3	1	8
4	2	8	1	9	3	5	6	7
3	5	1	6	8	7	4	2	9
2	7	4	9	3	5	1	8	6
1	8	9	7	6	4	2	5	3
5	3	6	2	1	8	7	9	4

PUZZLE 156

5	6	2	9	3	8	1	4	7
4	8	1	6	7	2	5	3	9
9	3	7	4	1	5	2	6	8
8	2	4	1	5	3	9	7	6
6	5	9	2	4	7	3	8	1
7	1	3	8	6	9	4	5	2
3	9	5	7	8	1	6	2	4
1	4	8	5	2	6	7	9	3
2	7	6	3	9	4	8	1	5

Answers

PUZZLE 167

8	4	2	5	1	7	9	3	6
3	9	1	6	4	2	7	5	8
5	7	6	8	9	3	2	1	4
4	8	7	3	6	1	5	2	9
1	2	3	9	8	5	4	6	7
9	6	5	7	2	4	3	8	1
7	1	4	2	3	8	6	9	5
2	5	9	1	7	6	8	4	3
6	3	8	4	5	9	1	7	2

PUZZLE 158

2	6	3	5	7	9	4	8	1
9	1	4	8	6	2	7	3	5
8	5	7	1	3	4	9	2	6
3	7	5	6	2	8	1	4	9
4	9	6	3	5	1	2	7	8
1	2	8	9	4	7	5	6	3
5	4	1	2	8	3	6	9	7
7	3	9	4	1	6	8	5	2
6	8	2	7	9	5	3	1	4

PUZZLE 159

2	5	1	4	6	3	8	7	9
9	6	8	7	1	2	5	4	3
7	4	3	9	8	5	1	6	2
4	7	5	2	3	9	6	1	8
1	9	6	8	7	4	2	3	5
3	8	2	1	5	6	7	9	4
6	1	9	3	2	8	4	5	7
8	3	7	5	4	1	9	2	6
5	2	4	6	9	7	3	8	1

PUZZLE 160

8	9	6	4	2	1	3	5	7
4	7	1	9	5	3	2	8	6
2	5	3	6	8	7	4	9	1
7	4	8	5	1	2	6	3	9
9	6	5	7	3	4	1	2	8
1	3	2	8	9	6	5	7	4
5	1	9	3	4	8	7	6	2
3	2	7	1	6	9	8	4	5
6	8	4	2	7	5	9	1	3

PUZZLE 161

7	4	5	6	9	8	1	2	3
1	6	8	3	7	2	4	5	9
9	2	3	1	5	4	7	8	6
6	8	1	9	4	7	2	3	5
2	3	7	5	6	1	9	4	8
4	5	9	2	8	3	6	7	1
3	7	2	8	1	9	5	6	4
5	9	4	7	3	6	8	1	2
8	1	6	4	2	5	3	9	7

PUZZLE 162

6	1	7	3	4	2	5	9	8
5	2	8	7	6	9	3	1	4
4	3	9	8	1	5	7	6	2
8	9	4	2	3	7	1	5	6
1	7	5	6	8	4	2	3	9
2	6	3	5	9	1	8	4	7
9	5	6	1	7	8	4	2	3
7	4	2	9	5	3	6	8	1
3	8	1	4	2	6	9	7	5

PUZZLE 163

5	6	4	7	1	8	2	3	9
3	8	1	9	5	2	7	4	6
2	7	9	4	6	3	1	8	5
8	9	3	5	2	4	6	1	7
4	5	7	6	8	1	3	9	2
1	2	6	3	7	9	4	5	8
6	1	2	8	4	5	9	7	3
9	4	5	2	3	7	8	6	1
7	3	8	1	9	6	5	2	4

PUZZLE 164

5	1	2	4	8	9	7	3	6
7	8	3	1	6	2	4	5	9
6	4	9	5	7	3	2	1	8
9	6	1	2	5	4	3	8	7
2	7	4	3	9	8	5	6	1
3	5	8	6	1	7	9	2	4
4	3	6	9	2	1	8	7	5
1	9	7	8	3	5	6	4	2
8	2	5	7	4	6	1	9	3

PUZZLE 165

7	8	3	4	6	1	9	2	5
6	4	9	7	2	5	1	8	3
2	5	1	8	3	9	6	7	4
4	7	5	9	1	8	2	3	6
3	9	8	2	4	6	7	5	1
1	2	6	5	7	3	4	9	8
9	3	2	6	5	4	8	1	7
5	6	7	1	8	2	3	4	9
8	1	4	3	9	7	5	6	2

PUZZLE 166

4	1	3	7	5	9	8	6	2
7	2	6	4	8	3	9	1	5
5	9	8	1	6	2	3	7	4
3	5	1	9	2	6	7	4	8
9	6	4	8	3	7	5	2	1
8	7	2	5	4	1	6	9	3
2	8	5	6	9	4	1	3	7
6	3	7	2	1	8	4	5	9
1	4	9	3	7	5	2	8	6

PUZZLE 167

1	9	6	3	2	5	8	4	7
2	4	8	7	1	6	3	5	9
5	7	3	8	4	9	2	1	6
4	1	7	9	5	2	6	8	3
8	2	9	6	3	1	5	7	4
3	6	5	4	7	8	9	2	1
6	3	1	5	8	4	7	9	2
9	8	4	2	6	7	1	3	5
7	5	2	1	9	3	4	6	8

PUZZLE 168

9	3	7	2	8	4	6	5	1
6	1	8	9	5	3	4	2	7
5	2	4	7	1	6	3	8	9
3	8	9	4	2	5	1	7	6
4	5	6	1	7	9	8	3	2
2	7	1	3	6	8	9	4	5
8	9	2	5	4	1	7	6	3
7	4	3	6	9	2	5	1	8
1	6	5	8	3	7	2	9	4

PUZZLE 169

5	1	8	7	4	6	2	3	9
6	7	3	2	8	9	4	5	1
4	9	2	5	3	1	7	8	6
8	2	6	9	5	3	1	4	7
9	5	1	4	2	7	3	6	8
7	3	4	1	6	8	9	2	5
2	8	7	6	9	4	5	1	3
1	6	5	3	7	2	8	9	4
3	4	9	8	1	5	6	7	2

PUZZLE 170

9	4	8	2	5	7	1	3	6
6	1	5	4	3	9	7	8	2
2	3	7	1	6	8	4	5	9
7	8	3	9	1	5	2	6	4
5	2	9	6	4	3	8	7	1
4	6	1	7	8	2	3	9	5
8	5	6	3	2	4	9	1	7
3	7	2	5	9	1	6	4	8
1	9	4	8	7	6	5	2	3

PUZZLE 171

1	3	5	8	6	4	2	9	7
8	7	4	9	3	2	6	1	5
6	2	9	5	7	1	8	4	3
7	5	1	6	2	3	9	8	4
3	9	6	7	4	8	1	5	2
4	8	2	1	9	5	7	3	6
5	6	7	4	8	9	3	2	1
9	1	3	2	5	6	4	7	8
2	4	8	3	1	7	5	6	9

PUZZLE 172

1	2	4	5	8	3	7	9	6
9	7	6	4	1	2	5	3	8
5	8	3	9	7	6	1	4	2
4	3	2	6	5	1	8	7	9
8	6	9	2	4	7	3	1	5
7	1	5	3	9	8	2	6	4
6	5	8	1	3	4	9	2	7
2	9	1	7	6	5	4	8	3
3	4	7	8	2	9	6	5	1

PUZZLE 173

5	6	1	7	3	4	9	8	2
4	7	2	8	9	1	5	6	3
9	3	8	2	6	5	4	1	7
7	4	6	3	1	2	8	9	5
1	2	5	6	8	9	7	3	4
3	8	9	5	4	7	6	2	1
6	5	3	4	2	8	1	7	9
8	1	4	9	7	3	2	5	6
2	9	7	1	5	6	3	4	8

PUZZLE 174

6	3	7	8	1	4	5	2	9
4	9	1	7	2	5	8	6	3
8	5	2	3	9	6	7	1	4
9	1	3	4	7	8	2	5	6
5	6	4	1	3	2	9	7	8
7	2	8	5	6	9	4	3	1
1	8	9	6	5	7	3	4	2
2	7	6	9	4	3	1	8	5
3	4	5	2	8	1	6	9	7

PUZZLE 175

7	4	6	8	3	2	5	9	1
5	2	1	7	6	9	8	3	4
9	8	3	5	4	1	7	6	2
4	3	9	1	2	7	6	8	5
8	1	7	6	5	4	3	2	9
2	6	5	3	9	8	1	4	7
1	7	4	9	8	6	2	5	3
3	9	8	2	1	5	4	7	6
6	5	2	4	7	3	9	1	8

PUZZLE 176

3	9	2	4	6	7	5	1	8
8	4	5	1	3	9	2	6	7
1	7	6	8	5	2	9	3	4
2	8	9	3	7	4	6	5	1
6	5	1	9	2	8	7	4	3
7	3	4	5	1	6	8	9	2
4	2	3	7	9	5	1	8	6
5	1	7	6	8	3	4	2	9
9	6	8	2	4	1	3	7	5

PUZZLE 177

3	8	1	6	2	4	7	5	9
4	6	9	1	5	7	2	8	3
5	2	7	9	3	8	1	6	4
9	4	6	3	7	1	8	2	5
2	1	3	8	6	5	4	9	7
8	7	5	2	4	9	3	1	6
7	9	2	4	8	6	5	3	1
1	5	8	7	9	3	6	4	2
6	3	4	5	1	2	9	7	8

PUZZLE 178

5	4	7	9	6	3	8	2	1
1	9	2	4	8	5	3	6	7
6	3	8	2	7	1	9	5	4
2	7	3	1	5	9	6	4	8
4	8	6	3	2	7	1	9	5
9	1	5	6	4	8	2	7	3
3	2	1	7	9	4	5	8	6
8	6	4	5	1	2	7	3	9
7	5	9	8	3	6	4	1	2

PUZZLE 179

5	8	9	3	4	2	7	6	1
1	3	6	9	7	8	5	2	4
2	7	4	5	1	6	8	3	9
6	1	7	4	2	5	9	8	3
4	2	3	6	8	9	1	7	5
9	5	8	7	3	1	6	4	2
7	6	2	1	5	3	4	9	8
8	9	5	2	6	4	3	1	7
3	4	1	8	9	7	2	5	6

PUZZLE 180

2	3	7	9	5	8	6	4	1
5	1	9	7	4	6	3	8	2
4	8	6	1	2	3	9	7	5
6	4	3	8	7	5	1	2	9
1	7	5	2	9	4	8	3	6
8	9	2	3	6	1	7	5	4
3	6	8	5	1	2	4	9	7
9	2	4	6	8	7	5	1	3
7	5	1	4	3	9	2	6	8

PUZZLE 181

3	8	2	1	4	5	6	7	9
1	9	7	6	8	3	4	2	5
5	6	4	9	2	7	8	3	1
9	3	8	7	5	4	2	1	6
4	1	5	2	6	8	3	9	7
2	7	6	3	9	1	5	4	8
7	2	9	8	3	6	1	5	4
8	5	3	4	1	9	7	6	2
6	4	1	5	7	2	9	8	3

PUZZLE 182

5	2	4	7	1	3	6	9	8
1	7	6	2	8	9	5	3	4
8	3	9	5	4	6	2	7	1
3	9	5	1	2	8	7	4	6
6	1	7	3	9	4	8	5	2
2	4	8	6	7	5	9	1	3
9	8	3	4	5	2	1	6	7
4	5	1	8	6	7	3	2	9
7	6	2	9	3	1	4	8	5

PUZZLE 183

4	9	1	2	5	3	8	6	7
5	8	3	6	1	7	2	9	4
6	7	2	9	8	4	3	5	1
9	6	4	1	7	2	5	3	8
2	3	5	8	4	6	7	1	9
8	1	7	3	9	5	4	2	6
3	4	6	7	2	1	9	8	5
7	2	9	5	6	8	1	4	3
1	5	8	4	3	9	6	7	2

PUZZLE 184

2	7	6	1	5	3	8	9	4
1	9	4	6	2	8	7	3	5
3	5	8	4	7	9	6	1	2
8	3	2	5	4	7	9	6	1
9	1	5	3	8	6	4	2	7
6	4	7	2	9	1	5	8	3
5	8	9	7	1	2	3	4	6
7	6	1	8	3	4	2	5	9
4	2	3	9	6	5	1	7	8

PUZZLE 184

1	6	5	3	7	4	8	9	2
7	9	2	6	8	5	4	1	3
3	4	8	1	2	9	7	6	5
8	3	1	7	9	2	6	5	4
4	2	6	8	5	1	9	3	7
5	7	9	4	3	6	1	2	8
6	1	3	2	4	7	5	8	9
9	8	7	5	1	3	2	4	6
2	5	4	9	6	8	3	7	1

PUZZLE 185

8	1	4	5	7	2	9	6	3
6	7	5	3	1	9	8	2	4
9	2	3	4	8	6	5	7	1
2	4	6	8	9	5	1	3	7
7	5	1	2	4	3	6	9	8
3	9	8	7	6	1	2	4	5
1	3	7	9	2	8	4	5	6
5	6	2	1	3	4	7	8	9
4	8	9	6	5	7	3	1	2

PUZZLE 186

6	8	9	7	1	4	2	5	3
4	2	7	3	8	5	1	6	9
1	3	5	9	6	2	4	8	7
7	5	8	1	4	9	6	3	2
2	1	3	8	5	6	9	7	4
9	4	6	2	3	7	8	1	5
3	6	2	5	9	8	7	4	1
5	7	4	6	2	1	3	9	8
8	9	1	4	7	3	5	2	6

PUZZLE 188

9	3	1	2	4	6	7	5	8
6	4	5	7	9	8	1	2	3
8	7	2	5	3	1	4	6	9
5	1	7	4	2	9	8	3	6
4	8	6	3	1	5	2	9	7
3	2	9	8	6	7	5	4	1
7	6	3	1	5	2	9	8	4
2	9	8	6	7	4	3	1	5
1	5	4	9	8	3	6	7	2

PUZZLE 189

1	7	9	6	3	8	4	2	5
2	5	8	4	7	9	6	1	3
6	3	4	5	2	1	7	8	9
9	2	5	3	1	6	8	7	4
4	6	7	8	9	5	2	3	1
3	8	1	2	4	7	9	5	6
5	4	3	7	6	2	1	9	8
7	9	6	1	8	3	5	4	2
8	1	2	9	5	4	3	6	7

PUZZLE 190

6	5	9	7	4	3	2	8	1
1	8	4	6	9	2	3	7	5
7	3	2	5	1	8	4	6	9
8	4	5	2	7	1	9	3	6
3	7	6	4	5	9	1	2	8
2	9	1	3	8	6	7	5	4
9	6	3	1	2	5	8	4	7
4	2	8	9	6	7	5	1	3
5	1	7	8	3	4	6	9	2

PUZZLE 191

4	5	6	3	7	1	2	8	9
1	9	2	8	6	5	7	4	3
7	8	3	2	4	9	6	1	5
8	3	5	4	2	6	9	7	1
6	4	1	9	8	7	3	5	2
2	7	9	1	5	3	8	6	4
9	2	7	6	1	4	5	3	8
3	6	4	5	9	8	1	2	7
5	1	8	7	3	2	4	9	6

PUZZLE 192

1	2	6	5	4	7	8	3	9
9	3	8	2	6	1	7	4	5
4	5	7	3	8	9	6	1	2
6	9	3	7	5	4	1	2	8
8	1	4	6	2	3	5	9	7
5	7	2	9	1	8	4	6	3
2	8	5	4	3	6	9	7	1
3	4	9	1	7	5	2	8	6
7	6	1	8	9	2	3	5	4

PUZZLE 193

9	7	3	2	4	6	5	8	1
2	5	8	7	1	9	4	6	3
1	6	4	5	3	8	9	2	7
6	2	7	9	5	4	1	3	8
8	4	9	1	2	3	7	5	6
3	1	5	8	6	7	2	4	9
5	9	1	3	8	2	6	7	4
7	3	6	4	9	5	8	1	2
4	8	2	6	7	1	3	9	5

PUZZLE 194

8	2	4	3	1	5	9	6	7
1	3	6	9	7	8	4	2	5
9	5	7	4	6	2	8	3	1
3	8	1	5	2	4	7	9	6
5	7	9	1	8	6	2	4	3
6	4	2	7	9	3	1	5	8
4	9	5	8	3	7	6	1	2
7	6	3	2	4	1	5	8	9
2	1	8	6	5	9	3	7	4

PUZZLE 195

2	1	3	9	8	4	7	5	6
4	7	6	2	5	1	9	8	3
5	8	9	3	6	7	4	2	1
8	2	5	6	9	3	1	4	7
9	3	1	4	7	5	8	6	2
7	6	4	1	2	8	5	3	9
6	5	8	7	3	9	2	1	4
3	4	7	8	1	2	6	9	5
1	9	2	5	4	6	3	7	8

PUZZLE 196

9	7	2	5	4	3	6	8	1
1	4	6	8	7	9	2	3	5
5	8	3	2	6	1	9	7	4
3	6	5	1	2	8	7	4	9
8	1	4	6	9	7	3	5	2
2	9	7	3	5	4	1	6	8
4	5	9	7	1	6	8	2	3
6	2	8	9	3	5	4	1	7
7	3	1	4	8	2	5	9	6

PUZZLE 197

5	1	9	3	8	2	4	6	7
6	4	8	5	7	9	2	3	1
3	2	7	1	4	6	5	8	9
8	6	5	9	3	4	1	7	2
4	7	3	2	1	8	9	5	6
1	9	2	6	5	7	3	4	8
9	3	1	8	6	5	7	2	4
2	8	4	7	9	3	6	1	5
7	5	6	4	2	1	8	9	3

PUZZLE 198

3	6	7	5	4	1	8	2	9
4	9	8	3	2	7	1	6	5
5	2	1	9	6	8	7	4	3
8	3	5	2	1	6	4	9	7
1	7	2	4	8	9	5	3	6
9	4	6	7	3	5	2	1	8
6	5	9	1	7	2	3	8	4
7	1	4	8	9	3	6	5	2
2	8	3	6	5	4	9	7	1

PUZZLE 199

9	7	4	5	1	8	3	6	2
8	2	3	6	4	9	5	7	1
5	6	1	3	2	7	4	8	9
1	4	6	9	3	2	8	5	7
2	8	9	7	5	4	1	3	6
7	3	5	1	8	6	2	9	4
6	5	2	8	7	1	9	4	3
4	9	8	2	6	3	7	1	5
3	1	7	4	9	5	6	2	8

PUZZLE 200

7	9	5	4	8	3	6	1	2
2	6	4	7	5	1	9	3	8
3	8	1	9	2	6	5	4	7
9	2	3	1	7	8	4	5	6
6	1	8	2	4	5	3	7	9
5	4	7	6	3	9	8	2	1
1	3	2	8	6	4	7	9	5
8	5	9	3	1	7	2	6	4
4	7	6	5	9	2	1	8	3

PUZZLE 201

6	8	1	2	4	7	5	3	9
2	3	4	1	5	9	7	6	8
9	5	7	8	6	3	1	2	4
4	9	6	5	3	8	2	7	1
3	1	8	9	7	2	6	4	5
5	7	2	4	1	6	8	9	3
7	6	5	3	9	1	4	8	2
8	4	9	6	2	5	3	1	7
1	2	3	7	8	4	9	5	6

PUZZLE 202

1	8	7	5	3	6	2	9	4
2	6	5	9	7	4	8	3	1
4	3	9	1	2	8	7	6	5
5	1	6	4	8	9	3	2	7
8	2	4	7	5	3	6	1	9
9	7	3	6	1	2	4	5	8
3	5	2	8	4	1	9	7	6
6	4	1	2	9	7	5	8	3
7	9	8	3	6	5	1	4	2

PUZZLE 203

8	3	6	9	2	1	5	7	4
7	2	1	8	4	5	9	3	6
5	4	9	3	6	7	2	1	8
4	7	5	6	8	3	1	9	2
3	1	8	5	9	2	4	6	7
6	9	2	7	1	4	3	8	5
1	8	7	4	5	9	6	2	3
2	5	3	1	7	6	8	4	9
9	6	4	2	3	8	7	5	1

PUZZLE 204

6	5	1	3	7	8	2	9	4
4	7	3	1	2	9	5	6	8
2	9	8	5	4	6	7	3	1
1	4	5	9	6	3	8	7	2
7	3	9	2	8	1	4	5	6
8	2	6	7	5	4	3	1	9
9	8	7	6	3	2	1	4	5
3	6	2	4	1	5	9	8	7
5	1	4	8	9	7	6	2	3

PUZZLE 205

9	4	8	1	7	3	2	6	5
6	7	1	5	2	9	3	4	8
2	5	3	4	6	8	7	9	1
7	3	9	2	8	1	4	5	6
4	6	2	3	9	5	8	1	7
1	8	5	6	4	7	9	2	3
8	1	7	9	5	2	6	3	4
3	2	6	7	1	4	5	8	9
5	9	4	8	3	6	1	7	2

PUZZLE 206

1	6	9	8	5	7	3	2	4
4	5	7	3	1	2	6	9	8
2	3	8	6	9	4	1	5	7
7	1	5	9	3	6	8	4	2
9	8	2	7	4	1	5	3	6
3	4	6	5	2	8	9	7	1
6	2	3	1	7	5	4	8	9
5	7	1	4	8	9	2	6	3
8	9	4	2	6	3	7	1	5

PUZZLE 207

4	7	2	1	5	3	9	6	8
9	6	8	7	4	2	5	1	3
3	5	1	9	6	8	2	7	4
1	9	4	5	8	7	6	3	2
2	8	6	3	1	4	7	5	9
7	3	5	2	9	6	8	4	1
5	4	7	8	3	9	1	2	6
8	1	3	6	2	5	4	9	7
6	2	9	4	7	1	3	8	5

PUZZLE 208

3	4	9	6	2	7	8	1	5
7	1	5	9	8	3	6	2	4
6	2	8	4	1	5	7	3	9
8	6	2	5	4	9	3	7	1
9	3	1	7	6	8	5	4	2
5	7	4	2	3	1	9	8	6
2	5	3	1	7	6	4	9	8
4	9	7	8	5	2	1	6	3
1	8	6	3	9	4	2	5	7

PUZZLE 209

5	6	3	4	2	8	7	1	9
1	4	8	7	6	9	2	3	5
7	9	2	5	1	3	8	6	4
4	7	1	6	3	2	9	5	8
2	3	5	9	8	4	6	7	1
6	8	9	1	5	7	3	4	2
8	5	7	2	4	6	1	9	3
3	1	6	8	9	5	4	2	7
9	2	4	3	7	1	5	8	6

PUZZLE 210

9	6	4	7	3	5	1	2	8
8	5	1	2	9	4	7	3	6
3	7	2	6	8	1	4	9	5
2	1	8	9	7	6	5	4	3
7	3	6	5	4	8	9	1	2
5	4	9	3	1	2	6	8	7
6	2	3	1	5	9	8	7	4
1	8	5	4	2	7	3	6	9
4	9	7	8	6	3	2	5	1

PUZZLE 211

1	2	7	8	5	4	6	3	9
4	6	5	7	3	9	2	1	8
8	3	9	2	1	6	7	5	4
2	5	4	3	6	8	1	9	7
3	8	1	9	7	2	4	6	5
7	9	6	5	4	1	3	8	2
6	1	8	4	2	5	9	7	3
9	7	2	6	8	3	5	4	1
5	4	3	1	9	7	8	2	6

PUZZLE 212

3	4	8	7	1	2	6	9	5
6	5	2	4	8	9	1	7	3
1	7	9	5	3	6	2	8	4
7	6	3	9	5	1	8	4	2
9	8	4	2	6	3	7	5	1
2	1	5	8	4	7	9	3	6
8	2	6	3	9	4	5	1	7
4	9	1	6	7	5	3	2	8
5	3	7	1	2	8	4	6	9

PUZZLE 213

7	6	2	8	1	9	3	5	4
9	3	4	7	2	5	8	1	6
8	5	1	6	4	3	2	9	7
6	4	9	5	7	8	1	2	3
3	1	7	9	6	2	5	4	8
5	2	8	1	3	4	7	6	9
1	9	3	2	8	6	4	7	5
2	8	5	4	9	7	6	3	1
4	7	6	3	5	1	9	8	2

PUZZLE 214

9	3	2	1	5	8	6	4	7
8	1	6	2	7	4	5	9	3
5	4	7	9	3	6	1	8	2
2	7	4	3	6	9	8	5	1
6	9	5	8	1	7	2	3	4
1	8	3	4	2	5	9	7	6
4	2	9	6	8	3	7	1	5
7	6	8	5	4	1	3	2	9
3	5	1	7	9	2	4	6	8

PUZZLE 215

5	7	3	4	1	6	9	2	8
8	1	2	5	9	3	7	6	4
9	4	6	7	8	2	3	5	1
2	8	4	6	7	5	1	3	9
1	9	5	3	2	8	4	7	6
6	3	7	1	4	9	5	8	2
4	5	1	2	6	7	8	9	3
3	6	9	8	5	1	2	4	7
7	2	8	9	3	4	6	1	5

PUZZLE 216

7	4	1	3	5	8	6	2	9
5	6	2	9	1	4	3	7	8
8	3	9	2	7	6	4	1	5
1	5	4	7	2	3	9	8	6
2	8	6	4	9	5	7	3	1
9	7	3	6	8	1	2	5	4
4	2	7	8	9	5	1	6	3
3	1	8	4	6	2	5	9	7
6	9	5	1	3	7	8	4	2

PUZZLE 218

5	8	3	2	7	4	6	1	9
1	9	2	5	6	3	4	8	7
4	6	7	8	1	9	2	5	3
9	1	4	7	5	8	3	2	6
3	2	5	1	4	6	9	7	8
6	7	8	9	3	2	1	4	5
2	5	6	3	8	1	7	9	4
8	3	9	4	2	7	5	6	1
7	4	1	6	9	5	8	3	2

PUZZLE 218

6	1	8	5	3	7	4	9	2
2	5	9	6	8	4	7	3	1
3	7	4	1	9	2	6	8	5
7	3	2	4	5	8	1	6	9
9	4	6	7	1	3	5	2	8
1	8	5	2	6	9	3	7	4
5	2	1	9	7	6	8	4	3
8	9	7	3	4	5	2	1	6
4	6	3	8	2	1	9	5	7

PUZZLE 219

5	2	9	3	6	4	8	1	7
8	4	7	1	9	5	6	3	2
3	6	1	2	7	8	9	4	5
9	3	2	7	4	6	5	8	1
4	8	6	5	3	1	7	2	9
1	7	5	8	2	9	3	6	4
2	9	8	4	5	3	1	7	6
6	1	4	9	8	7	2	5	3
7	5	3	6	1	2	4	9	8

PUZZLE 220

7	4	1	3	9	5	2	6	8
3	8	5	2	6	7	4	9	1
6	2	9	4	1	8	3	5	7
5	3	4	1	8	9	6	7	2
2	9	7	6	3	4	1	8	5
1	6	8	5	7	2	9	4	3
9	5	2	7	4	3	8	1	6
8	1	3	9	5	6	7	2	4
4	7	6	8	2	1	5	3	9

PUZZLE 221

9	2	1	8	4	3	7	6	5
3	8	5	2	6	7	9	4	1
7	6	4	5	9	1	2	8	3
5	1	8	7	2	4	6	3	9
6	7	9	3	5	8	1	2	4
4	3	2	6	1	9	5	7	8
2	4	6	9	8	5	3	1	7
8	9	3	1	7	6	4	5	2
1	5	7	4	3	2	8	9	6

PUZZLE 222

4	5	1	7	8	9	3	6	2
3	9	8	6	5	2	7	4	1
7	2	6	3	1	4	9	8	5
5	4	3	2	7	1	8	9	6
6	1	2	9	3	8	4	5	7
8	7	9	4	6	5	1	2	3
1	3	4	5	9	6	2	7	8
9	6	7	8	2	3	5	1	4
2	8	5	1	4	7	6	3	9

PUZZLE 223

7	9	1	5	4	2	3	8	6
6	4	2	8	9	3	1	5	7
3	5	8	7	6	1	2	4	9
5	3	7	4	1	9	6	2	8
1	6	9	2	8	5	4	7	3
8	2	4	6	3	7	9	1	5
2	8	3	9	5	4	7	6	1
9	7	6	1	2	8	5	3	4
4	1	5	3	7	6	8	9	2

PUZZLE 224

4	8	3	5	6	9	2	7	1
1	7	9	2	3	4	8	5	6
5	2	6	8	7	1	9	4	3
8	6	5	4	9	3	1	2	7
9	4	7	1	2	6	3	8	5
2	3	1	7	5	8	6	9	4
7	1	4	3	8	2	5	6	9
6	5	8	9	1	7	4	3	2
3	9	2	6	4	5	7	1	8

PUZZLE 225

8	3	2	1	7	5	6	4	9
5	1	7	9	4	6	2	3	8
4	9	6	2	8	3	7	5	1
1	2	8	4	6	9	5	7	3
9	4	3	5	1	7	8	6	2
6	7	5	3	2	8	1	9	4
2	5	1	7	9	4	3	8	6
7	6	9	8	3	2	4	1	5
3	8	4	6	5	1	9	2	7

PUZZLE 226

9	6	7	8	1	4	3	2	5
3	5	8	6	9	2	1	4	7
1	4	2	3	7	5	6	9	8
6	8	4	1	5	7	9	3	2
2	9	5	4	8	3	7	6	1
7	3	1	2	6	9	8	5	4
5	1	9	7	2	6	4	8	3
8	2	3	9	4	1	5	7	6
4	7	6	5	3	8	2	1	9

PUZZLE 227

3	1	4	8	6	2	5	9	7
9	7	8	4	5	3	6	2	1
2	5	6	9	7	1	3	4	8
6	3	7	1	2	5	4	8	9
1	4	9	7	3	8	2	5	6
8	2	5	6	4	9	7	1	3
7	6	1	5	8	4	9	3	2
4	8	3	2	9	6	1	7	5
5	9	2	3	1	7	8	6	4

PUZZLE 228

8	9	2	7	1	5	6	4	3
5	6	7	4	8	3	2	1	9
4	3	1	6	2	9	5	8	7
1	5	9	2	6	7	8	3	4
3	4	6	1	5	8	9	7	2
2	7	8	9	3	4	1	5	6
6	2	4	8	7	1	3	9	5
7	1	5	3	9	2	4	6	8
9	8	3	5	4	6	7	2	1

PUZZLE 229

7	5	6	9	2	8	1	3	4
1	3	2	5	4	7	6	8	9
4	9	8	6	3	1	2	5	7
2	8	5	3	6	9	4	7	1
6	1	9	7	5	4	8	2	3
3	7	4	8	1	2	9	6	5
9	2	3	1	7	6	5	4	8
8	6	7	4	9	5	3	1	2
5	4	1	2	8	3	7	9	6

PUZZLE 230

9	5	7	3	4	6	8	1	2
2	4	1	5	8	7	3	6	9
6	3	8	9	1	2	4	7	5
1	8	2	7	6	4	5	9	3
3	7	6	2	9	5	1	8	4
4	9	5	8	3	1	7	2	6
5	6	4	1	2	8	9	3	7
8	2	9	4	7	3	6	5	1
7	1	3	6	5	9	2	4	8

PUZZLE 231

8	9	4	3	2	6	5	7	1
2	7	6	5	4	1	9	8	3
5	3	1	8	7	9	4	2	6
7	4	8	2	5	3	6	1	9
9	1	5	4	6	7	8	3	2
3	6	2	1	9	8	7	5	4
1	2	9	7	8	4	3	6	5
6	8	3	9	1	5	2	4	7
4	5	7	6	3	2	1	9	8

PUZZLE 232

2	5	1	3	7	8	9	6	4
6	4	8	2	5	9	1	3	7
7	3	9	1	6	4	8	5	2
1	6	7	8	4	3	2	9	5
4	8	3	5	9	2	6	7	1
9	2	5	7	1	6	3	4	8
5	1	2	9	3	7	4	8	6
3	7	6	4	8	1	5	2	9
8	9	4	6	2	5	7	1	3

PUZZLE 233

3	6	1	9	7	5	4	8	2
2	7	5	3	8	4	9	1	6
9	8	4	6	1	2	3	5	7
1	5	9	8	3	7	2	6	4
6	4	8	5	2	9	1	7	3
7	2	3	4	6	1	8	9	5
8	9	7	2	4	6	5	3	1
4	3	6	1	5	8	7	2	9
5	1	2	7	9	3	6	4	8

PUZZLE 234

2	4	3	5	7	8	1	9	6
6	7	5	4	9	1	8	2	3
8	9	1	2	6	3	4	5	7
9	8	7	1	4	6	5	3	2
1	3	4	9	5	2	6	7	8
5	2	6	8	3	7	9	4	1
4	6	2	3	1	9	7	8	5
3	1	9	7	8	5	2	6	4
7	5	8	6	2	4	3	1	9

PUZZLE 235

7	2	9	3	8	1	5	6	4
5	4	8	6	7	2	3	1	9
3	1	6	9	5	4	8	2	7
6	5	4	7	3	8	1	9	2
8	9	1	4	2	6	7	5	3
2	3	7	1	9	5	6	4	8
1	6	3	8	4	9	2	7	5
9	7	5	2	6	3	4	8	1
4	8	2	5	1	7	9	3	6

PUZZLE 236

4	8	3	7	2	9	1	5	6
5	6	2	1	4	8	9	7	3
7	1	9	3	5	6	4	2	8
8	2	6	5	9	1	7	3	4
9	3	4	8	7	2	6	1	5
1	5	7	6	3	4	8	9	2
2	7	1	4	6	3	5	8	9
3	4	8	9	1	5	2	6	7
6	9	5	2	8	7	3	4	1

PUZZLE 237

4	8	5	7	9	1	3	2	6
7	3	9	2	5	6	8	1	4
1	6	2	3	4	8	9	5	7
9	4	1	6	3	5	7	8	2
3	7	8	4	1	2	5	6	9
5	2	6	9	8	7	1	4	3
6	5	7	8	2	9	4	3	1
2	1	3	5	7	4	6	9	8
8	9	4	1	6	3	2	7	5

PUZZLE 238

8	9	4	7	1	2	3	6	5
7	5	2	3	9	6	4	8	1
1	3	6	4	5	8	7	2	9
9	2	7	6	3	1	8	5	4
3	4	5	8	2	7	1	9	6
6	1	8	9	4	5	2	3	7
5	8	3	1	7	9	6	4	2
4	7	9	2	6	3	5	1	8
2	6	1	5	8	4	9	7	3

PUZZLE 239

6	5	3	8	7	1	9	2	4
8	1	4	9	2	3	6	5	7
7	2	9	4	6	5	8	1	3
5	7	8	1	9	6	4	3	2
2	9	1	5	3	4	7	8	6
4	3	6	2	8	7	5	9	1
1	8	5	6	4	2	3	7	9
3	4	2	7	5	9	1	6	8
9	6	7	3	1	8	2	4	5

PUZZLE 240

7	2	1	5	8	9	6	4	3
4	5	3	2	7	6	8	1	9
8	9	6	3	4	1	7	5	2
1	4	2	8	6	3	9	7	5
9	6	5	7	1	4	2	3	8
3	8	7	9	5	2	4	6	1
6	1	9	4	2	5	3	8	7
2	7	4	1	3	8	5	9	6
5	3	8	6	9	7	1	2	4

PUZZLE 241

4	7	1	2	9	3	6	8	5
6	5	9	4	7	8	3	2	1
3	2	8	5	6	1	9	7	4
9	4	2	1	8	5	7	3	6
1	3	6	7	4	9	8	5	2
7	8	5	3	2	6	1	4	9
2	9	4	8	1	7	5	6	3
5	1	7	6	3	2	4	9	8
8	6	3	9	5	4	2	1	7

PUZZLE 242

7	8	2	4	6	3	9	1	5
3	1	9	2	8	5	7	6	4
4	5	6	7	1	9	8	3	2
8	2	7	5	3	4	1	9	6
1	3	4	8	9	6	2	5	7
9	6	5	1	7	2	4	8	3
2	9	1	3	5	7	6	4	8
5	4	8	6	2	1	3	7	9
6	7	3	9	4	8	5	2	1

PUZZLE 243

3	2	4	9	5	8	1	6	7
9	1	6	4	2	7	3	5	8
5	8	7	1	6	3	2	9	4
8	9	3	6	4	2	5	7	1
7	5	1	8	3	9	4	2	6
6	4	2	5	7	1	9	8	3
4	7	8	3	9	5	6	1	2
2	3	9	7	1	6	8	4	5
1	6	5	2	8	4	7	3	9

PUZZLE 244

4	1	3	6	7	8	5	2	9
8	2	5	1	4	9	3	6	7
6	9	7	3	5	2	1	4	8
2	8	4	9	3	5	6	7	1
7	3	1	2	8	6	4	9	5
9	5	6	7	1	4	8	3	2
1	7	2	8	6	3	9	5	4
3	4	9	5	2	1	7	8	6
5	6	8	4	9	7	2	1	3

PUZZLE 245

6	8	2	5	7	4	1	9	3
4	7	3	1	8	9	2	6	5
9	5	1	2	6	3	7	8	4
5	2	7	8	4	1	6	3	9
8	9	6	3	5	7	4	1	2
3	1	4	9	2	6	8	5	7
1	6	5	4	9	2	3	7	8
2	3	9	7	1	8	5	4	6
7	4	8	6	3	5	9	2	1

PUZZLE 246

2	1	9	7	8	6	3	5	4
8	4	3	5	9	2	1	6	7
6	7	5	3	1	4	9	8	2
5	6	7	9	4	3	2	1	8
4	2	8	1	6	5	7	3	9
9	3	1	8	2	7	5	4	6
3	5	6	4	7	9	8	2	1
1	9	4	2	3	8	6	7	5
7	8	2	6	5	1	4	9	3

PUZZLE 247

8	9	3	6	4	5	2	7	1
1	4	6	3	7	2	9	5	8
7	5	2	9	8	1	3	6	4
4	8	1	5	3	6	7	2	9
9	3	7	4	2	8	5	1	6
2	6	5	1	9	7	8	4	3
6	1	8	2	5	9	4	3	7
3	2	9	7	6	4	1	8	5
5	7	4	8	1	3	6	9	2

PUZZLE 248

1	8	7	4	9	3	2	6	5
4	6	5	1	2	8	9	7	3
9	2	3	5	7	6	4	1	8
7	1	2	8	4	9	3	5	6
8	5	6	3	1	2	7	9	4
3	4	9	6	5	7	8	2	1
5	9	8	7	3	1	6	4	2
2	3	1	9	6	4	5	8	7
6	7	4	2	8	5	1	3	9

PUZZLE 249

4	6	9	7	8	5	3	2	1
2	7	8	1	6	3	9	4	5
1	3	5	9	2	4	7	6	8
7	8	3	2	4	9	5	1	6
6	9	1	5	7	8	2	3	4
5	4	2	6	3	1	8	9	7
9	2	7	4	5	6	1	8	3
8	1	4	3	9	7	6	5	2
3	5	6	8	1	2	4	7	9

PUZZLE 250

2	6	4	1	7	5	9	8	3
3	7	1	8	9	2	6	4	5
5	8	9	6	4	3	1	7	2
7	5	8	9	3	6	4	2	1
4	3	2	5	1	8	7	6	9
1	9	6	4	2	7	5	3	8
6	4	5	2	8	1	3	9	7
8	1	7	3	6	9	2	5	4
9	2	3	7	5	4	8	1	6

PUZZLE 251

8	7	3	1	5	6	2	9	4
5	9	2	8	3	4	1	7	6
4	1	6	7	9	2	8	5	3
3	4	1	9	6	8	5	2	7
2	5	9	3	7	1	4	6	8
7	6	8	2	4	5	3	1	9
6	8	5	4	1	7	9	3	2
1	3	4	6	2	9	7	8	5
9	2	7	5	8	3	6	4	1

PUZZLE 252

2	6	9	1	3	4	5	7	8
7	5	1	2	6	8	3	4	9
3	8	4	5	9	7	6	2	1
4	1	8	7	2	6	9	5	3
5	3	2	4	8	9	7	1	6
6	9	7	3	1	5	2	8	4
1	7	5	6	4	3	8	9	2
8	2	3	9	5	1	4	6	7
9	4	6	8	7	2	1	3	5

PUZZLE 253

2	1	4	6	7	8	3	5	9
8	7	9	1	5	3	6	4	2
3	5	6	2	9	4	8	7	1
4	6	8	3	2	5	9	1	7
1	3	7	9	4	6	5	2	8
5	9	2	8	1	7	4	3	6
7	2	3	5	6	9	1	8	4
9	8	1	4	3	2	7	6	5
6	4	5	7	8	1	2	9	3

PUZZLE 254

8	5	1	4	7	3	6	9	2
2	9	3	8	1	6	7	4	5
6	7	4	9	5	2	3	1	8
3	2	8	7	4	5	9	6	1
5	4	7	6	9	1	2	8	3
9	1	6	3	2	8	4	5	7
4	8	9	1	3	7	5	2	6
1	3	5	2	6	9	8	7	4
7	6	2	5	8	4	1	3	9

PUZZLE 255

7	3	1	8	6	9	4	2	5
5	9	4	3	2	1	8	7	6
8	2	6	7	5	4	3	1	9
6	8	3	9	1	5	7	4	2
4	7	9	2	3	6	1	5	8
1	5	2	4	7	8	6	9	3
2	1	8	6	9	7	5	3	4
9	4	5	1	8	3	2	6	7
3	6	7	5	4	2	9	8	1

PUZZLE 256

7	2	8	5	4	3	9	6	1
9	6	5	8	1	2	3	4	7
1	4	3	7	9	6	2	8	5
6	7	4	1	3	9	8	5	2
3	8	1	2	6	5	7	9	4
2	5	9	4	8	7	1	3	6
4	9	7	6	2	8	5	1	3
8	1	2	3	5	4	6	7	9
5	3	6	9	7	1	4	2	8

PUZZLE 257

3	6	7	1	2	4	8	5	9
8	5	1	9	3	7	4	2	6
2	4	9	6	8	5	3	1	7
7	1	3	8	9	6	2	4	5
9	2	5	4	7	3	6	8	1
4	8	6	2	5	1	9	7	3
5	7	4	3	6	8	1	9	2
1	3	2	5	4	9	7	6	8
6	9	8	7	1	2	5	3	4

PUZZLE 258

1	8	5	2	3	6	4	9	7
7	4	3	8	9	1	5	2	6
2	9	6	4	7	5	8	1	3
5	2	8	3	1	4	7	6	9
6	1	4	7	8	9	2	3	5
3	7	9	5	6	2	1	4	8
9	3	7	1	4	8	6	5	2
8	5	1	6	2	3	9	7	4
4	6	2	9	5	7	3	8	1

PUZZLE 259

5	8	3	1	4	9	6	2	7
9	7	1	6	2	3	8	5	4
2	4	6	5	7	8	9	1	3
7	1	2	8	5	4	3	9	6
6	9	4	7	3	2	5	8	1
3	5	8	9	6	1	7	4	2
4	6	9	2	8	7	1	3	5
8	2	5	3	1	6	4	7	9
1	3	7	4	9	5	2	6	8

PUZZLE 260

3	5	8	9	1	2	7	4	6
7	4	9	5	3	6	1	2	8
2	1	6	7	8	4	3	9	5
5	8	2	1	6	3	9	7	4
6	9	3	4	7	5	2	8	1
1	7	4	8	2	9	6	5	3
4	3	7	2	5	1	8	6	9
9	2	1	6	4	8	5	3	7
8	6	5	3	9	7	4	1	2

PUZZLE 261

4	2	1	5	9	6	8	7	3
5	9	7	3	2	8	1	6	4
8	3	6	4	7	1	2	5	9
7	4	9	8	3	2	6	1	5
2	6	5	9	1	4	3	8	7
3	1	8	7	6	5	9	4	2
9	8	3	6	5	7	4	2	1
1	7	4	2	8	3	5	9	6
6	5	2	1	4	9	7	3	8

PUZZLE 262

7	3	6	1	4	2	5	8	9
8	4	9	3	5	6	1	7	2
1	2	5	7	8	9	4	3	6
3	6	8	4	9	1	2	5	7
9	5	2	6	7	3	8	4	1
4	1	7	8	2	5	6	9	3
2	8	4	9	6	7	3	1	5
5	9	3	2	1	8	7	6	4
6	7	1	5	3	4	9	2	8

PUZZLE 263

3	1	6	5	7	9	2	4	8
2	9	5	1	4	8	6	7	3
8	4	7	6	3	2	1	9	5
5	6	2	3	9	7	4	8	1
9	7	4	8	5	1	3	6	2
1	3	8	4	2	6	9	5	7
4	8	9	7	1	3	5	2	6
7	5	3	2	6	4	8	1	9
6	2	1	9	8	5	7	3	4

PUZZLE 264

1	8	9	5	7	2	3	6	4
4	3	2	8	6	9	7	1	5
6	5	7	3	1	4	9	2	8
8	2	1	6	3	5	4	7	9
9	4	3	7	2	1	8	5	6
5	7	6	4	9	8	2	3	1
2	9	4	1	5	3	6	8	7
7	1	8	2	4	6	5	9	3
3	6	5	9	8	7	1	4	2

PUZZLE 265

9	3	6	4	1	2	5	8	7
5	2	1	8	9	7	3	6	4
7	8	4	6	3	5	2	9	1
6	4	3	7	2	9	1	5	8
1	9	8	5	6	4	7	3	2
2	7	5	1	8	3	9	4	6
3	6	9	2	7	8	4	1	5
4	1	7	3	5	6	8	2	9
8	5	2	9	4	1	6	7	3

PUZZLE 266

3	7	9	1	6	2	8	5	4
4	6	8	9	5	3	1	7	2
2	5	1	7	8	4	6	3	9
9	8	3	6	2	1	7	4	5
5	2	6	4	7	9	3	1	8
7	1	4	5	3	8	9	2	6
1	3	2	8	4	6	5	9	7
6	9	5	2	1	7	4	8	3
8	4	7	3	9	5	2	6	1

PUZZLE 267

2	6	9	1	5	4	8	3	7
5	4	3	7	8	2	1	6	9
8	1	7	3	6	9	4	2	5
4	8	1	2	9	5	3	7	6
7	5	6	4	3	8	9	1	2
9	3	2	6	7	1	5	8	4
3	9	8	5	2	7	6	4	1
6	7	4	9	1	3	2	5	8
1	2	5	8	4	6	7	9	3

PUZZLE 268

8	4	1	5	7	9	2	6	3
3	7	2	6	4	1	8	5	9
6	5	9	3	8	2	7	1	4
2	6	4	9	3	7	1	8	5
9	3	5	1	6	8	4	2	7
1	8	7	2	5	4	9	3	6
7	9	6	8	2	3	5	4	1
4	2	3	7	1	5	6	9	8
5	1	8	4	9	6	3	7	2

PUZZLE 269

6	5	4	9	7	1	2	8	3
1	8	9	4	2	3	6	7	5
7	3	2	8	5	6	4	1	9
3	9	1	2	6	5	8	4	7
2	7	6	3	4	8	5	9	1
5	4	8	7	1	9	3	6	2
9	6	7	5	3	4	1	2	8
4	2	3	1	8	7	9	5	6
8	1	5	6	9	2	7	3	4

PUZZLE 270

5	4	3	6	8	2	9	7	1
7	1	2	9	3	5	8	6	4
8	6	9	1	4	7	5	3	2
3	2	5	4	7	9	1	8	6
1	7	4	3	6	8	2	9	5
6	9	8	2	5	1	3	4	7
2	3	1	7	9	6	4	5	8
4	5	6	8	1	3	7	2	9
9	8	7	5	2	4	6	1	3

PUZZLE 271

2	4	7	3	8	9	1	5	6
8	3	5	1	7	6	2	4	9
6	1	9	5	2	4	8	7	3
9	2	4	6	5	1	7	3	8
1	5	3	7	4	8	9	6	2
7	8	6	2	9	3	5	1	4
4	9	1	8	6	5	3	2	7
3	7	8	4	1	2	6	9	5
5	6	2	9	3	7	4	8	1

PUZZLE 272

3	6	8	5	1	4	7	9	2
4	5	1	7	9	2	3	6	8
7	2	9	3	6	8	4	5	1
8	3	5	6	4	9	1	2	7
2	7	6	1	5	3	8	4	9
9	1	4	2	8	7	5	3	6
5	8	2	9	3	1	6	7	4
6	4	7	8	2	5	9	1	3
1	9	3	4	7	6	2	8	5

PUZZLE 273

5	3	7	1	4	9	8	2	6
2	1	9	5	8	6	3	7	4
4	6	8	2	3	7	9	5	1
8	2	6	9	5	4	7	1	3
7	4	1	3	6	8	2	9	5
3	9	5	7	2	1	4	6	8
1	7	3	8	9	5	6	4	2
6	5	2	4	7	3	1	8	9
9	8	4	6	1	2	5	3	7

PUZZLE 274

5	7	4	3	9	2	1	8	6
2	3	6	1	5	8	4	9	7
8	1	9	7	4	6	3	2	5
6	2	7	9	1	3	8	5	4
1	8	5	4	6	7	2	3	9
9	4	3	2	8	5	7	6	1
4	5	1	8	3	9	6	7	2
3	6	2	5	7	1	9	4	8
7	9	8	6	2	4	5	1	3

PUZZLE 275

3	4	2	1	6	8	5	7	9
5	7	1	3	9	2	8	6	4
9	6	8	5	4	7	3	1	2
7	1	6	9	8	3	4	2	5
8	3	5	4	2	1	6	9	7
2	9	4	6	7	5	1	8	3
1	2	7	8	3	4	9	5	6
6	5	3	7	1	9	2	4	8
4	8	9	2	5	6	7	3	1

PUZZLE 276

5	8	1	6	2	9	4	3	7
3	4	2	5	7	8	6	9	1
7	6	9	4	3	1	5	8	2
6	9	7	1	5	4	8	2	3
8	2	5	7	6	3	1	4	9
4	1	3	8	9	2	7	6	5
1	3	4	9	8	5	2	7	6
2	5	6	3	4	7	9	1	8
9	7	8	2	1	6	3	5	4

PUZZLE 277

1	4	7	6	2	8	3	9	5
5	2	9	7	4	3	1	6	8
3	8	6	5	1	9	7	2	4
4	7	3	8	9	1	2	5	6
2	6	1	4	7	5	9	8	3
8	9	5	2	3	6	4	7	1
7	3	8	1	5	2	6	4	9
9	5	2	3	6	4	8	1	7
6	1	4	9	8	7	5	3	2

PUZZLE 278

1	5	3	7	9	2	4	6	8
7	2	8	5	4	6	9	1	3
9	6	4	8	3	1	5	2	7
3	7	5	9	6	8	1	4	2
4	9	6	2	1	7	8	3	5
8	1	2	4	5	3	7	9	6
2	4	7	6	8	9	3	5	1
6	3	9	1	7	5	2	8	4
5	8	1	3	2	4	6	7	9

PUZZLE 279

5	7	6	3	1	9	8	4	2
8	3	4	2	5	7	6	9	1
2	9	1	6	4	8	7	5	3
6	4	7	1	9	2	3	8	5
3	1	5	8	6	4	2	7	9
9	2	8	5	7	3	4	1	6
4	5	9	7	3	6	1	2	8
1	6	2	4	8	5	9	3	7
7	8	3	9	2	1	5	6	4

PUZZLE 280

2	5	6	3	7	8	4	9	1
7	4	1	6	2	9	3	5	8
9	8	3	1	4	5	7	2	6
6	9	8	5	3	4	1	7	2
4	3	7	2	8	1	5	6	9
5	1	2	7	9	6	8	3	4
8	7	5	9	1	2	6	4	3
3	2	4	8	6	7	9	1	5
1	6	9	4	5	3	2	8	7

PUZZLE 281

1	9	6	2	8	4	5	3	7
2	4	5	9	3	7	1	8	6
8	3	7	1	5	6	2	4	9
5	1	9	8	7	2	4	6	3
6	8	4	3	1	5	7	9	2
3	7	2	4	6	9	8	5	1
7	6	3	5	4	1	9	2	8
9	5	8	7	2	3	6	1	4
4	2	1	6	9	8	3	7	5

PUZZLE 282

2	3	8	4	9	1	5	6	7
7	9	4	6	8	5	3	1	2
6	1	5	2	3	7	8	9	4
5	7	3	9	1	4	2	8	6
8	6	1	3	7	2	4	5	9
9	4	2	5	6	8	1	7	3
1	5	6	7	4	3	9	2	8
4	2	9	8	5	6	7	3	1
3	8	7	1	2	9	6	4	5

PUZZLE 283

6	4	8	2	3	9	1	7	5
7	3	2	1	6	5	4	8	9
9	1	5	8	4	7	6	3	2
3	6	1	5	9	4	8	2	7
4	5	7	3	2	8	9	1	6
2	8	9	7	1	6	3	5	4
1	9	3	6	7	2	5	4	8
5	7	4	9	8	3	2	6	1
8	2	6	4	5	1	7	9	3

PUZZLE 284

4	8	6	2	3	5	9	1	7
1	7	2	9	4	8	6	5	3
5	9	3	6	7	1	8	4	2
2	1	4	3	8	6	5	7	9
9	6	5	1	2	7	4	3	8
7	3	8	5	9	4	1	2	6
6	2	9	4	5	3	7	8	1
8	5	1	7	6	2	3	9	4
3	4	7	8	1	9	2	6	5

PUZZLE 285

9	6	2	4	1	5	8	7	3
3	7	8	2	6	9	1	4	5
1	5	4	3	8	7	6	9	2
7	9	5	8	4	2	3	1	6
4	8	6	1	7	3	2	5	9
2	3	1	9	5	6	4	8	7
6	4	7	5	2	8	9	3	1
5	1	9	6	3	4	7	2	8
8	2	3	7	9	1	5	6	4

PUZZLE 286

9	6	4	1	2	8	5	7	3
5	1	2	3	7	6	8	4	9
7	8	3	4	9	5	6	1	2
4	9	7	5	1	3	2	8	6
1	3	8	6	4	2	9	5	7
6	2	5	7	8	9	4	3	1
3	4	6	9	5	7	1	2	8
2	5	9	8	3	1	7	6	4
8	7	1	2	6	4	3	9	5

PUZZLE 287

6	9	1	5	7	3	8	4	2
4	3	8	9	2	1	7	5	6
7	2	5	6	8	4	1	3	9
1	4	3	2	6	7	5	9	8
8	6	9	3	4	5	2	7	1
2	5	7	1	9	8	4	6	3
3	7	2	8	5	6	9	1	4
5	8	6	4	1	9	3	2	7
9	1	4	7	3	2	6	8	5

PUZZLE 288

6	2	1	5	9	3	7	4	8
4	9	3	6	8	7	2	1	5
5	7	8	1	4	2	9	6	3
7	8	6	9	2	5	1	3	4
9	1	4	3	7	6	5	8	2
3	5	2	8	1	4	6	9	7
2	3	9	4	5	1	8	7	6
8	6	7	2	3	9	4	5	1
1	4	5	7	6	8	3	2	9

PUZZLE 289

1	5	8	9	4	2	7	3	6
3	6	9	5	8	7	4	1	2
2	4	7	6	3	1	8	5	9
7	3	2	4	1	9	6	8	5
9	1	6	8	7	5	2	4	3
4	8	5	3	2	6	9	7	1
5	7	4	2	9	3	1	6	8
8	2	3	1	6	4	5	9	7
6	9	1	7	5	8	3	2	4

PUZZLE 290

3	4	8	9	2	6	7	5	1
6	1	5	8	3	7	2	4	9
2	9	7	5	1	4	3	8	6
1	7	9	6	8	2	5	3	4
5	2	6	1	4	3	9	7	8
4	8	3	7	9	5	1	6	2
9	6	1	3	7	8	4	2	5
7	5	4	2	6	9	8	1	3
8	3	2	4	5	1	6	9	7

PUZZLE 291

8	3	1	2	9	6	4	5	7
9	5	2	1	7	4	8	3	6
7	6	4	5	3	8	9	1	2
5	4	6	8	2	9	3	7	1
1	2	8	7	4	3	6	9	5
3	9	7	6	1	5	2	4	8
2	7	9	4	6	1	5	8	3
6	8	3	9	5	7	1	2	4
4	1	5	3	8	2	7	6	9

PUZZLE 292

7	5	9	1	2	6	4	3	8
2	3	4	9	8	7	6	1	5
6	1	8	5	4	3	7	2	9
4	2	7	3	9	5	8	6	1
1	9	5	8	6	2	3	4	7
8	6	3	4	7	1	9	5	2
5	7	1	6	3	8	2	9	4
3	4	2	7	1	9	5	8	6
9	8	6	2	5	4	1	7	3

PUZZLE 293

7	5	8	2	4	1	3	9	6
4	9	6	7	8	3	2	1	5
1	2	3	9	6	5	7	4	8
8	4	9	6	1	2	5	3	7
3	6	5	4	9	7	1	8	2
2	1	7	3	5	8	9	6	4
9	8	2	1	7	6	4	5	3
6	7	1	5	3	4	8	2	9
5	3	4	8	2	9	6	7	1

PUZZLE 294

6	1	8	2	7	5	3	9	4
3	9	2	8	4	1	6	5	7
7	4	5	6	9	3	8	1	2
9	3	6	7	1	8	2	4	5
2	7	1	5	3	4	9	8	6
5	8	4	9	6	2	7	3	1
8	6	3	4	5	7	1	2	9
4	2	7	1	8	9	5	6	3
1	5	9	3	2	6	4	7	8

PUZZLE295

4	1	9	6	5	2	3	7	8
3	6	8	7	1	4	5	2	9
2	5	7	9	3	8	1	4	6
8	3	5	4	2	1	6	9	7
7	2	4	5	6	9	8	1	3
6	9	1	3	8	7	4	5	2
9	7	6	1	4	3	2	8	5
1	8	3	2	7	5	9	6	4
5	4	2	8	9	6	7	3	1

PUZZLE 296

3	4	6	8	7	9	5	2	1
5	2	9	3	1	6	8	7	4
1	7	8	5	4	2	6	3	9
7	8	1	4	2	5	9	6	3
9	3	2	1	6	7	4	8	5
4	6	5	9	8	3	2	1	7
2	9	4	7	3	8	1	5	6
6	5	7	2	9	1	3	4	8
8	1	3	6	5	4	7	9	2

PUZZLE 297

8	6	4	2	5	9	1	3	7
9	5	3	1	4	7	8	6	2
7	1	2	8	6	3	4	5	9
2	4	6	5	7	8	3	9	1
3	8	5	6	9	1	7	2	4
1	7	9	4	3	2	5	8	6
4	3	7	9	2	5	6	1	8
6	2	8	3	1	4	9	7	5
5	9	1	7	8	6	2	4	3

PUZZLE 298

1	9	2	8	6	7	3	5	4
6	4	5	9	3	1	7	8	2
8	3	7	2	4	5	1	9	6
4	2	8	3	1	9	5	6	7
7	5	3	6	2	4	9	1	8
9	1	6	7	5	8	2	4	3
3	7	4	1	9	6	8	2	5
5	8	1	4	7	2	6	3	9
2	6	9	5	8	3	4	7	1

PUZZLE 299

5	1	3	9	6	4	2	8	7
7	9	8	5	2	1	4	3	6
6	4	2	3	7	8	1	9	5
2	6	9	7	4	5	8	1	3
8	5	7	1	9	3	6	2	4
4	3	1	6	8	2	5	7	9
9	7	4	8	1	6	3	5	2
1	2	5	4	3	7	9	6	8
3	8	6	2	5	9	7	4	1

PUZZLE 300

2	6	1	9	7	3	8	4	5
8	4	5	1	2	6	3	9	7
3	7	9	8	5	4	1	6	2
5	3	8	4	1	9	7	2	6
9	1	7	6	3	2	5	8	4
6	2	4	5	8	7	9	1	3
1	5	3	2	6	8	4	7	9
4	8	2	7	9	5	6	3	1
7	9	6	3	4	1	2	5	8

PUZZLE 301

7	6	3	8	9	1	4	5	2
5	8	9	7	2	4	1	6	3
2	1	4	3	5	6	8	9	7
3	5	1	9	4	7	2	8	6
8	7	6	5	3	2	9	4	1
4	9	2	6	1	8	7	3	5
9	2	5	4	7	3	6	1	8
6	3	7	1	8	9	5	2	4
1	4	8	2	6	5	3	7	9

PUZZLE 302

4	1	7	8	6	5	9	3	2
9	5	8	7	3	2	4	6	1
2	3	6	1	9	4	5	7	8
7	6	4	3	8	9	2	1	5
5	2	9	4	1	7	6	8	3
3	8	1	2	5	6	7	9	4
6	4	3	9	2	8	1	5	7
8	7	5	6	4	1	3	2	9
1	9	2	5	7	3	8	4	6

PUZZLE 303

8	9	1	2	3	6	5	7	4
5	3	7	4	8	9	2	6	1
6	2	4	1	5	7	9	3	8
4	5	9	6	2	3	8	1	7
7	8	2	9	1	4	3	5	6
1	6	3	8	7	5	4	2	9
9	4	5	7	6	2	1	8	3
3	1	6	5	4	8	7	9	2
2	7	8	3	9	1	6	4	5

PUZZLE 304

6	2	4	5	8	9	7	1	3
9	7	1	3	2	4	8	5	6
3	8	5	1	6	7	4	2	9
2	9	7	6	3	8	5	4	1
8	5	6	4	1	2	9	3	7
1	4	3	7	9	5	2	6	8
7	6	2	8	4	3	1	9	5
5	3	9	2	7	1	6	8	4
4	1	8	9	5	6	3	7	2

PUZZLE 305

2	4	9	3	1	5	7	6	8
8	5	7	9	6	4	3	2	1
3	1	6	2	7	8	9	5	4
7	8	3	4	2	9	6	1	5
9	2	1	5	8	6	4	3	7
4	6	5	7	3	1	2	8	9
6	3	4	1	5	7	8	9	2
1	7	8	6	9	2	5	4	3
5	9	2	8	4	3	1	7	6

PUZZLE 306

9	3	4	6	7	5	8	1	2
2	5	1	9	3	8	6	7	4
8	7	6	2	4	1	3	9	5
6	2	7	8	5	9	4	3	1
5	9	3	4	1	2	7	6	8
4	1	8	7	6	3	5	2	9
3	4	2	1	8	6	9	5	7
1	8	5	3	9	7	2	4	6
7	6	9	5	2	4	1	8	3

PUZZLE 307

7	6	8	9	4	3	1	2	5
5	3	9	1	7	2	8	6	4
1	4	2	5	6	8	3	9	7
8	2	1	4	3	7	9	5	6
4	5	3	6	9	1	2	7	8
6	9	7	8	2	5	4	1	3
3	7	4	2	5	9	6	8	1
9	8	6	7	1	4	5	3	2
2	1	5	3	8	6	7	4	9

PUZZLE 308

4	6	7	5	9	2	1	8	3
5	2	8	4	3	1	9	7	6
3	9	1	7	8	6	5	2	4
7	5	9	1	6	4	2	3	8
6	4	3	9	2	8	7	1	5
8	1	2	3	5	7	4	6	9
9	7	4	8	1	3	6	5	2
1	3	6	2	4	5	8	9	7
2	8	5	6	7	9	3	4	1

PUZZLE 309

5	2	6	4	1	7	9	3	8
8	1	3	9	5	2	6	7	4
7	9	4	8	3	6	5	1	2
4	3	9	6	2	1	8	5	7
1	8	5	7	4	3	2	9	6
6	7	2	5	8	9	3	4	1
9	6	8	1	7	5	4	2	3
3	4	7	2	9	8	1	6	5
2	5	1	3	6	4	7	8	9

PUZZLE 310

9	8	6	2	1	7	5	4	3
1	5	7	3	4	8	9	2	6
3	4	2	9	5	6	1	7	8
7	2	8	1	9	3	6	5	4
5	3	9	6	7	4	2	8	1
6	1	4	5	8	2	3	9	7
4	6	1	8	2	9	7	3	5
8	9	3	7	6	5	4	1	2
2	7	5	4	3	1	8	6	9

PUZZLE 311

7	9	8	3	1	6	2	4	5
4	2	5	9	8	7	6	3	1
3	6	1	5	2	4	9	8	7
2	4	3	6	9	5	1	7	8
8	5	6	2	7	1	3	9	4
9	1	7	8	4	3	5	2	6
5	3	2	7	6	8	4	1	9
6	7	4	1	3	9	8	5	2
1	8	9	4	5	2	7	6	3

PUZZLE 312

4	1	5	8	6	7	3	9	2
9	2	8	5	3	1	7	6	4
6	7	3	4	2	9	1	5	8
2	3	4	9	7	5	6	8	1
8	9	1	6	4	3	2	7	5
7	5	6	1	8	2	4	3	9
5	4	9	3	1	6	8	2	7
3	8	2	7	5	4	9	1	6
1	6	7	2	9	8	5	4	3

Answers

PUZZLE 313

7	5	9	8	1	3	4	2	6
2	8	3	5	4	6	9	1	7
6	1	4	7	2	9	3	8	5
8	6	2	9	5	7	1	4	3
5	4	1	2	3	8	6	7	9
3	9	7	1	6	4	8	5	2
9	3	5	4	7	1	2	6	8
4	2	8	6	9	5	7	3	1
1	7	6	3	8	2	5	9	4

PUZZLE 314

4	5	9	2	6	7	3	8	1
1	6	7	8	9	3	2	5	4
2	8	3	4	5	1	9	7	6
6	3	1	7	2	8	5	4	9
7	4	8	5	1	9	6	3	2
9	2	5	3	4	6	8	1	7
5	7	4	6	8	2	1	9	3
3	1	6	9	7	5	4	2	8
8	9	2	1	3	4	7	6	5

PUZZLE 315

8	6	4	9	7	1	3	5	2
5	2	3	4	8	6	1	9	7
9	1	7	2	3	5	8	6	4
1	4	5	6	2	3	7	8	9
7	9	2	1	4	8	6	3	5
6	3	8	5	9	7	2	4	1
4	5	1	8	6	2	9	7	3
2	7	6	3	5	9	4	1	8
3	8	9	7	1	4	5	2	6

PUZZLE 316

6	7	3	8	1	5	9	4	2
2	8	5	9	7	4	6	1	3
1	4	9	2	3	6	5	7	8
3	2	7	5	9	1	8	6	4
5	6	8	7	4	2	1	3	9
9	1	4	6	8	3	2	5	7
4	3	2	1	5	8	7	9	6
8	9	1	4	6	7	3	2	5
7	5	6	3	2	9	4	8	1

PUZZLE 317

6	5	8	2	4	1	9	7	3
4	7	1	8	3	9	6	2	5
3	9	2	6	5	7	1	4	8
8	2	9	5	6	4	3	1	7
5	6	3	1	7	8	2	9	4
1	4	7	9	2	3	5	8	6
9	1	5	7	8	6	4	3	2
2	8	4	3	1	5	7	6	9
7	3	6	4	9	2	8	5	1

PUZZLE 318

5	9	1	2	6	7	3	8	4
8	3	2	5	4	9	7	1	6
6	4	7	1	3	8	2	9	5
4	7	8	9	1	6	5	3	2
3	1	6	4	2	5	9	7	8
9	2	5	8	7	3	6	4	1
1	6	4	3	9	2	8	5	7
2	5	9	7	8	4	1	6	3
7	8	3	6	5	1	4	2	9

PUZZLE 319

4	5	1	2	8	6	7	9	3
8	6	3	9	1	7	2	4	5
7	2	9	4	5	3	1	6	8
5	3	6	8	2	4	9	7	1
9	4	7	1	6	5	3	8	2
2	1	8	7	3	9	4	5	6
6	8	4	3	7	1	5	2	9
1	9	5	6	4	2	8	3	7
3	7	2	5	9	8	6	1	4

PUZZLE 320

8	2	4	7	6	3	1	5	9
1	3	5	9	4	8	6	2	7
9	7	6	2	5	1	8	4	3
4	8	7	1	3	9	5	6	2
5	1	9	6	7	2	3	8	4
2	6	3	5	8	4	9	7	1
6	5	2	3	1	7	4	9	8
7	4	1	8	9	6	2	3	5
3	9	8	4	2	5	7	1	6

PUZZLE 321

9	2	5	8	6	4	3	7	1
8	3	7	2	5	1	6	9	4
6	4	1	9	7	3	5	2	8
3	6	9	7	1	2	8	4	5
1	8	2	5	4	6	9	3	7
7	5	4	3	9	8	2	1	6
5	1	6	4	3	9	7	8	2
4	9	8	6	2	7	1	5	3
2	7	3	1	8	5	4	6	9

PUZZLE 322

4	7	8	9	5	2	6	3	1
5	1	6	7	8	3	4	2	9
3	2	9	4	1	6	5	8	7
2	8	3	5	9	4	7	1	6
6	5	7	2	3	1	9	4	8
1	9	4	8	6	7	2	5	3
9	6	1	3	4	5	8	7	2
8	4	2	1	7	9	3	6	5
7	3	5	6	2	8	1	9	4

PUZZLE 323

1	4	2	7	9	5	8	6	3
3	6	9	8	2	1	4	7	5
8	5	7	4	6	3	9	1	2
7	1	5	3	4	8	6	2	9
4	2	6	1	5	9	7	3	8
9	3	8	6	7	2	5	4	1
5	8	4	2	1	6	3	9	7
6	9	1	5	3	7	2	8	4
2	7	3	9	8	4	1	5	6

PUZZLE 324

4	5	2	3	1	8	6	7	9
6	3	7	4	2	9	5	1	8
9	8	1	7	6	5	3	4	2
2	1	8	5	9	6	7	3	4
3	7	6	1	8	4	2	9	5
5	9	4	2	3	7	1	8	6
8	2	3	6	4	1	9	5	7
7	6	9	8	5	3	4	2	1
1	4	5	9	7	2	8	6	3

PUZZLE 325

2	3	5	1	8	9	4	7	6
9	6	8	2	4	7	3	1	5
4	1	7	6	3	5	8	2	9
8	7	2	4	5	3	9	6	1
6	4	9	8	1	2	7	5	3
3	5	1	9	7	6	2	4	8
1	9	3	5	2	4	6	8	7
7	8	4	3	6	1	5	9	2
5	2	6	7	9	8	1	3	4

PUZZLE 326

4	9	5	7	6	8	1	2	3
6	3	1	9	5	2	7	8	4
2	7	8	3	1	4	6	5	9
5	4	9	8	7	1	3	6	2
7	1	3	6	2	9	8	4	5
8	2	6	5	4	3	9	1	7
9	5	7	2	8	6	4	3	1
3	6	4	1	9	5	2	7	8
1	8	2	4	3	7	5	9	6

PUZZLE 327

2	8	3	4	7	1	5	6	9
5	4	1	8	6	9	7	3	2
9	6	7	2	5	3	1	4	8
4	1	5	3	9	2	8	7	6
6	3	9	7	1	8	2	5	4
8	7	2	5	4	6	3	9	1
7	2	4	6	8	5	9	1	3
3	9	6	1	2	7	4	8	5
1	5	8	9	3	4	6	2	7

PUZZLE 328

4	7	1	6	8	2	3	9	5
6	9	8	5	1	3	2	4	7
2	3	5	7	4	9	6	1	8
7	5	2	1	3	6	4	8	9
9	1	3	4	2	8	7	5	6
8	4	6	9	5	7	1	3	2
3	8	7	2	9	4	5	6	1
1	2	4	8	6	5	9	7	3
5	6	9	3	7	1	8	2	4

PUZZLE 329

5	1	6	3	8	4	7	2	9
9	2	8	1	7	5	6	4	3
7	3	4	2	9	6	1	8	5
2	8	7	5	6	3	9	1	4
3	4	9	8	1	2	5	6	7
6	5	1	7	4	9	2	3	8
4	7	3	9	2	1	8	5	6
1	9	5	6	3	8	4	7	2
8	6	2	4	5	7	3	9	1

PUZZLE 330

4	7	8	5	1	9	6	3	2
9	5	6	2	8	3	7	4	1
3	1	2	4	6	7	5	8	9
6	8	4	3	9	2	1	5	7
1	9	5	8	7	4	3	2	6
7	2	3	6	5	1	8	9	4
2	4	1	7	3	8	9	6	5
8	6	7	9	2	5	4	1	3
5	3	9	1	4	6	2	7	8

PUZZLE 331

6	1	3	4	9	7	2	5	8
7	4	8	2	5	3	9	6	1
9	2	5	1	6	8	3	4	7
1	6	2	9	4	5	7	8	3
8	5	9	7	3	1	6	2	4
3	7	4	8	2	6	1	9	5
2	8	6	3	1	4	5	7	9
5	3	7	6	8	9	4	1	2
4	9	1	5	7	2	8	3	6

PUZZLE 332

9	1	3	2	6	7	8	4	5
6	4	2	5	8	3	1	7	9
8	5	7	4	9	1	6	3	2
2	3	9	7	4	6	5	1	8
5	7	4	9	1	8	2	6	3
1	8	6	3	5	2	7	9	4
4	2	1	6	3	5	9	8	7
3	6	5	8	7	9	4	2	1
7	9	8	1	2	4	3	5	6

PUZZLE 333

2	5	1	7	6	3	4	9	8
7	9	6	5	4	8	1	3	2
8	4	3	9	1	2	6	5	7
9	1	2	4	5	7	8	6	3
5	3	7	6	8	9	2	4	1
4	6	8	2	3	1	5	7	9
3	2	5	8	7	4	9	1	6
1	8	4	3	9	6	7	2	5
6	7	9	1	2	5	3	8	4

PUZZLE 334

9	2	1	6	5	3	4	8	7
5	7	3	4	8	9	2	6	1
8	4	6	1	2	7	5	3	9
1	5	8	3	9	2	6	7	4
2	6	9	7	4	8	3	1	5
4	3	7	5	1	6	8	9	2
3	1	5	9	6	4	7	2	8
7	9	2	8	3	5	1	4	6
6	8	4	2	7	1	9	5	3

PUZZLE 335

3	1	7	4	5	6	8	2	9
4	6	8	2	9	1	5	3	7
9	2	5	3	7	8	1	6	4
6	4	1	7	3	9	2	5	8
2	7	3	1	8	5	4	9	6
8	5	9	6	4	2	7	1	3
1	8	2	9	6	7	3	4	5
5	9	4	8	1	3	6	7	2
7	3	6	5	2	4	9	8	1

PUZZLE 336

7	2	3	1	4	8	5	9	6
6	8	4	5	9	2	1	7	3
9	5	1	7	6	3	8	2	4
8	4	2	9	7	6	3	1	5
5	1	7	2	3	4	6	8	9
3	6	9	8	1	5	2	4	7
4	9	6	3	2	1	7	5	8
1	7	5	6	8	9	4	3	2
2	3	8	4	5	7	9	6	1

PUZZLE 337

4	6	2	1	7	5	9	8	3
7	8	5	3	9	6	1	4	2
9	1	3	2	4	8	5	6	7
1	3	6	9	2	7	4	5	8
2	7	9	5	8	4	3	1	6
8	5	4	6	3	1	7	2	9
6	2	7	4	5	9	8	3	1
3	4	8	7	1	2	6	9	5
5	9	1	8	6	3	2	7	4

PUZZLE 338

5	8	3	9	7	1	4	6	2
2	9	1	3	6	4	8	7	5
7	6	4	8	5	2	1	3	9
1	7	2	5	4	3	6	9	8
3	4	8	7	9	6	2	5	1
9	5	6	2	1	8	7	4	3
4	3	7	1	2	5	9	8	6
8	2	9	6	3	7	5	1	4
6	1	5	4	8	9	3	2	7

PUZZLE 339

5	9	3	7	6	4	2	8	1
1	7	2	9	5	8	4	6	3
4	6	8	2	1	3	9	7	5
2	1	9	5	4	6	8	3	7
3	4	7	8	9	1	5	2	6
8	5	6	3	2	7	1	9	4
6	2	5	1	3	9	7	4	8
9	8	4	6	7	5	3	1	2
7	3	1	4	8	2	6	5	9

PUZZLE 340

9	4	2	6	8	3	5	7	1
7	8	1	9	4	5	3	2	6
5	6	3	2	1	7	8	4	9
6	5	8	1	9	4	2	3	7
3	2	9	7	5	6	1	8	4
4	1	7	3	2	8	9	6	5
2	3	5	4	7	9	6	1	8
1	9	4	8	6	2	7	5	3
8	7	6	5	3	1	4	9	2

PUZZLE 341

3	9	8	4	2	6	1	5	7
6	1	5	3	8	7	9	4	2
4	2	7	5	9	1	8	6	3
1	3	2	8	5	9	6	7	4
5	7	9	6	4	3	2	8	1
8	6	4	7	1	2	5	3	9
7	5	1	9	3	8	4	2	6
2	4	6	1	7	5	3	9	8
9	8	3	2	6	4	7	1	5

PUZZLE 342

7	1	2	6	9	3	4	8	5
5	8	4	1	7	2	3	9	6
6	9	3	8	4	5	1	7	2
9	2	7	4	5	6	8	3	1
8	3	5	7	1	9	6	2	4
4	6	1	3	2	8	7	5	9
2	7	6	9	3	4	5	1	8
1	5	8	2	6	7	9	4	3
3	4	9	5	8	1	2	6	7

PUZZLE 343

3	4	8	5	9	1	7	2	6
1	2	7	8	4	6	9	3	5
6	9	5	7	2	3	4	1	8
5	7	4	1	6	9	2	8	3
9	1	6	2	3	8	5	4	7
2	8	3	4	7	5	1	6	9
7	6	1	9	8	2	3	5	4
4	3	2	6	5	7	8	9	1
8	5	9	3	1	4	6	7	2

PUZZLE 344

3	5	1	2	7	6	8	9	4
9	8	2	4	1	5	7	6	3
4	6	7	8	3	9	5	2	1
6	1	5	9	2	4	3	7	8
2	9	8	3	5	7	4	1	6
7	4	3	6	8	1	2	5	9
8	2	9	5	6	3	1	4	7
5	7	4	1	9	8	6	3	2
1	3	6	7	4	2	9	8	5

PUZZLE 345

4	6	3	9	2	1	7	5	8
1	2	7	8	5	6	9	4	3
5	8	9	4	7	3	6	1	2
8	9	1	5	4	2	3	6	7
7	4	6	3	9	8	1	2	5
3	5	2	1	6	7	4	8	9
6	7	8	2	1	9	5	3	4
9	3	5	6	8	4	2	7	1
2	1	4	7	3	5	8	9	6

PUZZLE 246

1	3	6	4	5	9	2	7	8
2	7	8	1	3	6	9	4	5
5	4	9	8	7	2	1	3	6
8	1	3	5	2	4	7	6	9
6	2	7	3	9	8	5	1	4
9	5	4	7	6	1	3	8	2
4	8	2	9	1	3	6	5	7
7	9	1	6	8	5	4	2	3
3	6	5	2	4	7	8	9	1

PUZZLE 247

2	1	8	7	6	3	5	4	9
5	6	3	8	9	4	1	2	7
4	7	9	1	2	5	8	6	3
6	9	2	5	1	8	3	7	4
7	3	5	6	4	2	9	8	1
1	8	4	9	3	7	2	5	6
3	4	1	2	8	6	7	9	5
9	2	7	4	5	1	6	3	8
8	5	6	3	7	9	4	1	2

PUZZLE 348

1	8	7	2	5	4	9	3	6
9	5	6	3	7	1	2	8	4
3	2	4	8	6	9	1	7	5
8	6	3	5	2	7	4	9	1
5	4	9	6	1	3	7	2	8
7	1	2	9	4	8	6	5	3
2	3	8	4	9	6	5	1	7
6	7	5	1	3	2	8	4	9
4	9	1	7	8	5	3	6	2

PUZZLE 349

```
9 5 1 6 2 8 3 7 4
8 4 7 1 3 9 2 6 5
2 3 6 5 7 4 1 8 9
3 7 2 8 9 5 6 4 1
4 1 8 2 6 7 5 9 3
5 6 9 4 1 3 8 2 7
1 8 5 9 4 2 7 3 6
6 9 3 7 8 1 4 5 2
7 2 4 3 5 6 9 1 8
```

PUZZLE 350

```
3 5 7 1 6 4 9 2 8
4 6 9 7 8 2 3 1 5
2 8 1 9 3 5 4 7 6
8 2 6 4 5 9 7 3 1
5 7 4 3 2 1 6 8 9
1 9 3 6 7 8 2 5 4
9 3 2 5 1 6 8 4 7
7 4 5 8 9 3 1 6 2
6 1 8 2 4 7 5 9 3
```

PUZZLE 351

```
6 8 2 7 4 5 3 9 1
7 3 1 9 6 2 8 4 5
4 5 9 1 8 3 6 7 2
8 6 5 2 9 7 1 3 4
9 7 4 6 3 1 2 5 8
1 2 3 8 5 4 9 6 7
3 1 7 5 2 9 4 8 6
2 9 6 4 7 8 5 1 3
5 4 8 3 1 6 7 2 9
```

PUZZLE 352

```
5 3 2 8 6 1 7 4 9
4 1 9 3 7 5 2 8 6
6 8 7 9 2 4 3 1 5
8 2 4 1 3 6 5 9 7
1 9 3 5 4 7 8 6 2
7 6 5 2 8 9 1 3 4
2 5 6 4 1 3 9 7 8
9 7 1 6 5 8 4 2 3
3 4 8 7 9 2 6 5 1
```

PUZZLE 353

```
6 8 9 5 1 4 3 2 7
3 5 2 8 7 9 4 1 6
7 4 1 3 2 6 8 9 5
2 3 7 4 6 8 1 5 9
5 9 8 1 3 7 2 6 4
1 6 4 2 9 5 7 8 3
8 7 5 6 4 2 9 3 1
9 1 6 7 8 3 5 4 2
4 2 3 9 5 1 6 7 8
```

PUZZLE 354

```
2 1 9 6 7 4 8 5 3
4 3 7 2 8 5 9 1 6
6 8 5 1 3 9 4 7 2
9 7 8 4 6 2 5 3 1
5 4 6 9 1 3 2 8 7
1 2 3 8 5 7 6 4 9
8 5 1 7 9 6 3 2 4
3 6 4 5 2 1 7 9 8
7 9 2 3 4 8 1 6 5
```

PUZZLE 355

```
9 8 1 2 7 6 4 3 5
6 4 7 1 3 5 9 8 2
5 3 2 9 4 8 6 7 1
7 6 9 8 1 4 5 2 3
8 5 4 3 2 7 1 6 9
2 1 3 6 5 9 8 4 7
3 9 8 7 6 1 2 5 4
4 2 6 5 9 3 7 1 8
1 7 5 4 8 2 3 9 6
```

PUZZLE 356

```
7 8 5 2 1 4 6 3 9
4 6 3 7 9 8 1 2 5
1 9 2 5 3 6 4 8 7
8 5 1 9 2 7 3 4 6
2 3 7 4 6 5 8 9 1
6 4 9 3 8 1 5 7 2
5 1 4 8 7 2 9 6 3
9 2 8 6 5 3 7 1 4
3 7 6 1 4 9 2 5 8
```

PUZZLE 357

```
2 1 4 5 8 6 3 7 9
5 6 9 2 3 7 8 4 1
3 7 8 9 4 1 6 5 2
1 3 7 8 6 5 2 9 4
4 9 2 7 1 3 5 8 6
8 5 6 4 9 2 7 1 3
6 2 5 1 7 9 4 3 8
9 8 3 6 5 4 1 2 7
7 4 1 3 2 8 9 6 5
```

PUZZLE 358

```
7 4 8 3 6 9 1 2 5
5 3 9 4 1 2 8 6 7
6 1 2 8 7 5 4 9 3
8 5 6 1 9 4 3 7 2
2 9 1 6 3 7 5 4 8
3 7 4 5 2 8 6 1 9
1 2 3 9 8 6 7 5 4
4 6 7 2 5 3 9 8 1
9 8 5 7 4 1 2 3 6
```

PUZZLE 359

```
9 3 4 7 5 1 8 6 2
8 5 7 6 2 9 4 3 1
1 2 6 8 4 3 7 9 5
5 6 1 9 7 8 3 2 4
2 7 3 4 6 5 9 1 8
4 8 9 1 3 2 5 7 6
6 4 5 3 1 7 2 8 9
3 9 2 5 8 6 1 4 7
7 1 8 2 9 4 6 5 3
```

PUZZLE 360

```
8 2 7 1 3 9 4 5 6
4 9 5 7 6 8 2 3 1
6 1 3 5 2 4 8 7 9
3 7 2 9 5 1 6 4 8
9 6 1 8 4 3 7 2 5
5 8 4 6 7 2 1 9 3
1 5 8 4 9 7 3 6 2
7 3 6 2 8 5 9 1 4
2 4 9 3 1 6 5 8 7
```

PUZZLE 361

6	3	7	5	4	1	2	9	8
9	4	1	2	3	8	6	7	5
8	2	5	6	7	9	4	1	3
5	9	3	7	1	6	8	2	4
7	6	8	4	2	3	1	5	9
4	1	2	8	9	5	3	6	7
3	7	6	9	8	2	5	4	1
1	5	4	3	6	7	9	8	2
2	8	9	1	5	4	7	3	6

PUZZLE 362

1	3	9	7	5	2	4	6	8
8	7	2	4	9	6	1	5	3
6	4	5	1	8	3	7	9	2
3	6	8	5	7	4	2	1	9
2	5	1	9	3	8	6	4	7
4	9	7	6	2	1	8	3	5
9	8	6	2	4	5	3	7	1
7	2	4	3	1	9	5	8	6
5	1	3	8	6	7	9	2	4

PUZZLE 363

6	9	1	5	7	2	4	3	8
7	8	5	3	6	4	2	9	1
4	3	2	9	1	8	7	6	5
5	7	3	4	8	9	6	1	2
8	6	4	2	5	1	3	7	9
2	1	9	6	3	7	5	8	4
9	5	7	1	4	3	8	2	6
1	4	8	7	2	6	9	5	3
3	2	6	8	9	5	1	4	7

PUZZLE 364

7	1	8	4	5	2	9	3	6
9	5	6	3	8	1	7	4	2
2	3	4	6	9	7	8	5	1
4	6	3	1	7	5	2	9	8
1	9	5	2	6	8	4	7	3
8	7	2	9	3	4	1	6	5
5	2	1	7	4	3	6	8	9
6	8	7	5	2	9	3	1	4
3	4	9	8	1	6	5	2	7

PUZZLE 365

5	8	7	3	6	2	4	1	9
6	4	9	5	7	1	2	8	3
1	3	2	8	9	4	6	7	5
4	5	3	1	8	9	7	6	2
2	7	8	4	5	6	9	3	1
9	1	6	2	3	7	8	5	4
8	6	4	9	1	3	5	2	7
7	9	1	6	2	5	3	4	8
3	2	5	7	4	8	1	9	6

PUZZLE 366

7	6	2	3	1	9	5	4	8
1	4	9	2	5	8	6	7	3
3	5	8	4	7	6	1	2	9
6	2	1	7	8	3	9	5	4
4	9	3	5	6	2	8	1	7
5	8	7	9	4	1	2	3	6
8	3	5	1	9	7	4	6	2
2	1	6	8	3	4	7	9	5
9	7	4	6	2	5	3	8	1

PUZZLE 367

3	4	2	9	8	5	6	7	1
5	9	7	6	1	3	2	8	4
1	8	6	4	2	7	5	9	3
2	6	4	7	3	8	1	5	9
8	1	5	2	9	4	3	6	7
9	7	3	5	6	1	4	2	8
4	2	9	3	7	6	8	1	5
6	5	8	1	4	9	7	3	2
7	3	1	8	5	2	9	4	6

PUZZLE 368

8	5	4	7	6	3	1	9	2
6	1	7	5	2	9	3	4	8
2	3	9	4	8	1	5	6	7
4	7	5	1	3	2	6	8	9
1	6	8	9	4	5	2	7	3
3	9	2	8	7	6	4	5	1
7	4	6	3	1	8	9	2	5
5	2	1	6	9	7	8	3	4
9	8	3	2	5	4	7	1	6

PUZZLE 369

6	8	9	7	4	3	1	2	5
2	1	4	8	5	6	9	3	7
5	3	7	1	2	9	8	6	4
3	9	8	6	7	4	5	1	2
1	6	2	5	3	8	4	7	9
4	7	5	2	9	1	3	8	6
7	2	3	4	1	5	6	9	8
9	5	6	3	8	2	7	4	1
8	4	1	9	6	7	2	5	3

PUZZLE 370

9	5	4	6	3	1	8	2	7
8	7	3	4	5	2	1	9	6
2	1	6	9	7	8	3	5	4
6	9	8	1	4	7	5	3	2
4	2	5	8	9	3	7	6	1
1	3	7	2	6	5	9	4	8
7	4	2	5	1	9	6	8	3
3	6	9	7	8	4	2	1	5
5	8	1	3	2	6	4	7	9

PUZZLE 371

4	7	9	8	1	6	5	3	2
2	1	6	9	5	3	4	7	8
8	5	3	7	2	4	9	1	6
5	6	7	3	9	8	1	2	4
1	9	2	6	4	5	3	8	7
3	8	4	2	7	1	6	9	5
9	3	8	4	6	2	7	5	1
6	2	1	5	3	7	8	4	9
7	4	5	1	8	9	2	6	3

PUZZLE 372

3	5	9	6	4	7	2	1	8
7	6	4	1	8	2	5	9	3
8	2	1	5	9	3	7	4	6
1	8	7	9	2	5	3	6	4
2	4	5	8	3	6	1	7	9
6	9	3	7	1	4	8	5	2
4	1	2	3	7	9	6	8	5
5	3	8	4	6	1	9	2	7
9	7	6	2	5	8	4	3	1

PUZZLE 373

5	6	1	4	8	2	9	7	3
7	2	9	1	6	3	8	4	5
8	4	3	7	5	9	2	6	1
6	8	4	2	3	7	5	1	9
3	5	7	8	9	1	4	2	6
9	1	2	5	4	6	7	3	8
4	3	6	9	7	8	1	5	2
1	7	8	6	2	5	3	9	4
2	9	5	3	1	4	6	8	7

PUZZLE 374

2	6	3	8	1	7	5	9	4
5	7	9	2	3	4	1	6	8
1	4	8	6	9	5	2	3	7
6	2	5	9	4	8	3	7	1
4	9	1	7	5	3	6	8	2
3	8	7	1	6	2	9	4	5
8	3	4	5	2	9	7	1	6
9	1	2	4	7	6	8	5	3
7	5	6	3	8	1	4	2	9

PUZZLE 375

9	1	4	2	7	6	3	5	8
8	2	5	4	3	1	7	6	9
7	6	3	8	9	5	2	4	1
6	4	1	3	8	7	9	2	5
2	5	9	1	6	4	8	7	3
3	7	8	9	5	2	4	1	6
5	8	6	7	4	9	1	3	2
1	9	7	6	2	3	5	8	4
4	3	2	5	1	8	6	9	7

PUZZLE 376

5	3	4	1	6	7	2	9	8
7	1	8	2	9	5	3	4	6
2	6	9	3	4	8	5	1	7
4	9	7	6	2	3	8	5	1
8	2	6	5	1	9	7	3	4
1	5	3	8	7	4	6	2	9
6	4	1	7	3	2	9	8	5
3	7	5	9	8	1	4	6	2
9	8	2	4	5	6	1	7	3

PUZZLE 377

1	2	9	4	6	3	7	5	8
3	6	8	9	7	5	4	2	1
4	5	7	8	1	2	3	9	6
7	9	6	3	2	4	8	1	5
2	8	3	1	5	7	6	4	9
5	1	4	6	9	8	2	7	3
8	4	5	7	3	1	9	6	2
6	7	1	2	8	9	5	3	4
9	3	2	5	4	6	1	8	7

PUZZLE 378

3	4	6	1	8	5	9	2	7
8	2	9	7	3	4	6	1	5
7	5	1	9	2	6	3	4	8
1	3	8	4	7	9	5	6	2
6	7	2	8	5	3	4	9	1
4	9	5	2	6	1	8	7	3
9	6	7	3	1	8	2	5	4
2	8	4	5	9	7	1	3	6
5	1	3	6	4	2	7	8	9

PUZZLE 379

4	5	8	2	9	3	6	7	1
2	3	7	1	6	5	4	9	8
6	1	9	4	8	7	5	3	2
7	2	5	6	3	8	1	4	9
9	6	1	5	7	4	2	8	3
8	4	3	9	1	2	7	6	5
3	7	6	8	2	1	9	5	4
1	9	4	3	5	6	8	2	7
5	8	2	7	4	9	3	1	6

PUZZLE 380

8	9	6	1	4	3	5	7	2
2	5	1	6	7	8	3	9	4
3	4	7	2	9	5	1	8	6
9	3	2	7	8	1	6	4	5
6	8	5	3	2	4	7	1	9
7	1	4	5	6	9	8	2	3
4	6	8	9	5	7	2	3	1
1	2	9	8	3	6	4	5	7
5	7	3	4	1	2	9	6	8

PUZZLE 381

8	6	2	9	1	3	5	7	4
9	4	3	8	5	7	2	1	6
5	7	1	2	4	6	8	3	9
4	3	6	7	8	2	1	9	5
1	2	9	5	6	4	7	8	3
7	8	5	1	3	9	6	4	2
6	9	7	4	2	1	3	5	8
3	5	4	6	7	8	9	2	1
2	1	8	3	9	5	4	6	7

PUZZLE 382

4	3	7	9	5	6	8	1	2
8	9	1	4	2	3	7	6	5
2	5	6	1	7	8	4	3	9
7	1	5	3	9	2	6	8	4
9	8	4	7	6	1	2	5	3
6	2	3	5	8	4	9	7	1
5	6	8	2	3	9	1	4	7
3	4	2	6	1	7	5	9	8
1	7	9	8	4	5	3	2	6

PUZZLE 383

4	8	1	2	6	5	7	9	3
9	2	6	8	3	7	1	5	4
7	3	5	1	9	4	2	8	6
8	4	9	3	2	6	5	1	7
1	5	3	7	8	9	4	6	2
2	6	7	4	5	1	9	3	8
6	1	4	9	7	8	3	2	5
5	9	2	6	4	3	8	7	1
3	7	8	5	1	2	6	4	9

PUZZLE 384

4	1	2	9	6	7	3	5	8
8	6	7	1	5	3	9	2	4
5	3	9	4	8	2	1	7	6
3	5	8	6	9	4	2	1	7
6	7	4	2	3	1	8	9	5
9	2	1	8	7	5	6	4	3
2	9	3	5	4	8	7	6	1
7	4	6	3	1	9	5	8	2
1	8	5	7	2	6	4	3	9

PUZZLE 385

7	9	6	2	3	5	1	8	4
5	4	1	9	8	7	6	3	2
2	8	3	6	4	1	9	5	7
3	6	4	7	1	9	5	2	8
9	5	8	3	2	4	7	1	6
1	2	7	8	5	6	3	4	9
8	1	9	5	7	2	4	6	3
4	7	2	1	6	3	8	9	5
6	3	5	4	9	8	2	7	1

PUZZLE 386

8	3	2	9	7	4	6	1	5
9	6	4	1	8	5	2	3	7
5	7	1	6	3	2	9	4	8
6	1	5	3	4	8	7	9	2
7	4	8	2	5	9	3	6	1
3	2	9	7	6	1	5	8	4
2	5	3	8	1	6	4	7	9
4	8	7	5	9	3	1	2	6
1	9	6	4	2	7	8	5	3

PUZZLE 387

5	2	3	8	9	4	7	1	6
9	6	7	3	1	5	8	2	4
1	8	4	7	6	2	5	3	9
3	4	5	1	2	8	9	6	7
8	7	2	9	3	6	4	5	1
6	1	9	5	4	7	3	8	2
7	5	6	4	8	1	2	9	3
2	9	8	6	7	3	1	4	5
4	3	1	2	5	9	6	7	8

PUZZLE 388

6	4	7	8	3	9	1	5	2
9	8	5	1	2	4	3	6	7
3	1	2	5	7	6	4	8	9
1	7	6	2	4	5	8	9	3
5	3	9	6	1	8	2	7	4
4	2	8	3	9	7	5	1	6
2	6	3	9	5	1	7	4	8
7	9	1	4	8	3	6	2	5
8	5	4	7	6	2	9	3	1

PUZZLE 389

8	4	7	6	9	3	2	5	1
5	6	2	7	1	8	9	3	4
9	1	3	4	5	2	7	6	8
6	8	5	2	3	1	4	7	9
2	3	4	9	8	7	6	1	5
1	7	9	5	6	4	3	8	2
4	2	6	8	7	5	1	9	3
3	9	8	1	2	6	5	4	7
7	5	1	3	4	9	8	2	6

PUZZLE 390

9	5	3	4	7	6	8	1	2
4	8	6	5	2	1	9	7	3
2	7	1	8	3	9	4	5	6
3	4	9	7	6	2	5	8	1
8	2	7	3	1	5	6	9	4
6	1	5	9	8	4	3	2	7
7	3	4	1	5	8	2	6	9
5	9	2	6	4	7	1	3	8
1	6	8	2	9	3	7	4	5

PUZZLE 391

6	4	8	7	9	1	2	3	5
7	9	2	6	5	3	8	4	1
3	1	5	8	4	2	9	7	6
8	6	9	5	1	4	3	2	7
5	3	1	2	7	8	4	6	9
2	7	4	3	6	9	1	5	8
4	8	7	1	3	6	5	9	2
1	5	3	9	2	7	6	8	4
9	2	6	4	8	5	7	1	3

PUZZLE 392

2	9	1	6	8	7	5	3	4
4	8	7	1	5	3	6	9	2
6	5	3	9	4	2	7	1	8
3	4	5	2	7	6	9	8	1
7	2	9	8	1	5	4	6	3
1	6	8	4	3	9	2	7	5
5	7	2	3	6	1	8	4	9
9	3	4	7	2	8	1	5	6
8	1	6	5	9	4	3	2	7

PUZZLE 393

5	6	4	2	3	9	7	1	8
2	7	1	4	6	8	5	3	9
8	3	9	1	5	7	6	2	4
6	5	8	3	9	1	2	4	7
7	1	2	8	4	5	3	9	6
9	4	3	6	7	2	8	5	1
1	2	6	5	8	4	9	7	3
4	8	7	9	2	3	1	6	5
3	9	5	7	1	6	4	8	2

PUZZLE 394

4	2	6	7	3	1	8	5	9
7	3	8	5	4	9	6	2	1
1	9	5	8	6	2	4	7	3
5	1	2	4	9	7	3	8	6
6	8	4	3	1	5	2	9	7
3	7	9	6	2	8	1	4	5
2	6	3	9	5	4	7	1	8
8	5	1	2	7	3	9	6	4
9	4	7	1	8	6	5	3	2

PUZZLE 395

8	1	7	9	5	4	6	3	2
5	3	2	6	7	1	4	8	9
9	4	6	3	2	8	5	7	1
1	8	4	5	6	3	2	9	7
2	7	3	4	8	9	1	5	6
6	5	9	2	1	7	8	4	3
4	6	5	7	3	2	9	1	8
7	2	1	8	9	5	3	6	4
3	9	8	1	4	6	7	2	5

PUZZLE 396

3	4	9	1	8	7	5	2	6
8	1	6	2	9	5	7	4	3
5	7	2	6	3	4	9	1	8
2	9	8	3	4	6	1	7	5
7	6	1	8	5	2	3	9	4
4	5	3	9	7	1	6	8	2
9	3	7	5	2	8	4	6	1
1	8	4	7	6	3	2	5	9
6	2	5	4	1	9	8	3	7

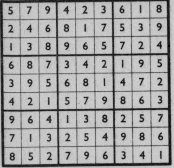

PUZZLE 397

5	7	9	4	2	3	6	1	8
2	4	6	8	1	7	5	3	9
1	3	8	9	6	5	7	2	4
6	8	7	3	4	2	1	9	5
3	9	5	6	8	1	4	7	2
4	2	1	5	7	9	8	6	3
9	6	4	1	3	8	2	5	7
7	1	3	2	5	4	9	8	6
8	5	2	7	9	6	3	4	1

PUZZLE 398

5	2	8	3	1	4	6	7	9
1	7	3	2	9	6	8	4	5
6	4	9	5	7	8	3	2	1
3	8	6	9	5	7	4	1	2
4	1	5	6	3	2	7	9	8
7	9	2	8	4	1	5	6	3
9	5	7	1	6	3	2	8	4
8	6	1	4	2	5	9	3	7
2	3	4	7	8	9	1	5	6

PUZZLE 399

1	8	9	7	4	6	2	3	5
2	4	6	3	8	5	7	1	9
5	3	7	9	2	1	8	4	6
9	5	2	4	6	3	1	7	8
8	7	3	5	1	9	6	2	4
6	1	4	2	7	8	5	9	3
4	6	8	1	3	7	9	5	2
7	2	5	6	9	4	3	8	1
3	9	1	8	5	2	4	6	7

PUZZLE 400

7	8	6	3	9	5	4	1	2
3	2	4	8	7	1	6	9	5
9	1	5	6	4	2	8	3	7
6	5	2	9	3	4	7	8	1
1	9	7	2	5	8	3	6	4
4	3	8	1	6	7	5	2	9
2	4	1	5	8	3	9	7	6
5	6	3	7	1	9	2	4	8
8	7	9	4	2	6	1	5	3

PUZZLE 401

6	5	1	3	9	7	2	4	8
8	9	3	2	4	5	1	6	7
2	7	4	8	6	1	5	3	9
9	6	7	5	1	2	3	8	4
5	4	2	6	8	3	7	9	1
3	1	8	4	7	9	6	2	5
1	8	5	9	2	6	4	7	3
7	2	9	1	3	4	8	5	6
4	3	6	7	5	8	9	1	2

PUZZLE 402

5	6	2	1	9	7	4	8	3
7	1	4	8	3	5	2	6	9
8	3	9	4	2	6	7	5	1
9	4	8	5	1	2	6	3	7
6	2	3	9	7	8	5	1	4
1	7	5	6	4	3	8	9	2
3	8	7	2	5	1	9	4	6
4	5	1	7	6	9	3	2	8
2	9	6	3	8	4	1	7	5

PUZZLE 403

5	9	6	7	3	8	1	2	4
8	7	4	5	2	1	3	6	9
1	3	2	6	4	9	5	7	8
4	2	8	3	1	7	9	5	6
9	5	3	4	6	2	8	1	7
6	1	7	8	9	5	2	4	3
3	6	5	2	8	4	7	9	1
2	4	1	9	7	3	6	8	5
7	8	9	1	5	6	4	3	2

PUZZLE 404

4	2	8	1	9	6	5	7	3
9	6	3	7	2	5	1	4	8
5	1	7	4	3	8	6	2	9
8	9	6	5	1	2	4	3	7
3	5	4	9	6	7	2	8	1
2	7	1	8	4	3	9	6	5
6	3	5	2	8	9	7	1	4
7	4	2	3	5	1	8	9	6
1	8	9	6	7	4	3	5	2

PUZZLE 405

2	6	9	5	4	3	7	8	1
4	7	8	1	2	9	6	5	3
1	5	3	6	7	8	9	2	4
3	4	5	2	8	7	1	6	9
8	9	6	4	5	1	2	3	7
7	2	1	9	3	6	8	4	5
9	1	2	3	6	4	5	7	8
5	3	7	8	1	2	4	9	6
6	8	4	7	9	5	3	1	2

PUZZLE 406

7	9	8	5	6	3	1	4	2
2	1	6	8	4	7	3	5	9
4	5	3	2	1	9	8	6	7
1	6	4	9	3	8	7	2	5
8	2	7	4	5	6	9	1	3
5	3	9	7	2	1	6	8	4
6	4	1	3	9	5	2	7	8
9	7	2	1	8	4	5	3	6
3	8	5	6	7	2	4	9	1

PUZZLE 407

5	7	3	9	2	8	1	4	6
1	2	4	7	6	5	3	8	9
6	9	8	4	3	1	5	2	7
4	5	1	2	8	7	6	9	3
7	3	9	6	1	4	8	5	2
8	6	2	3	5	9	4	7	1
2	8	5	1	9	6	7	3	4
3	4	6	5	7	2	9	1	8
9	1	7	8	4	3	2	6	5

PUZZLE 408

2	8	4	1	9	6	3	7	5
9	3	1	7	8	5	2	6	4
7	5	6	2	4	3	1	9	8
5	4	3	9	7	8	6	1	2
6	2	8	3	5	1	7	4	9
1	7	9	4	6	2	8	5	3
8	1	7	5	3	4	9	2	6
3	9	5	6	2	7	4	8	1
4	6	2	8	1	9	5	3	7

PUZZLE 409

```
8 7 2 6 4 3 9 1 5
9 1 3 2 8 5 4 7 6
4 6 5 9 7 1 8 3 2
7 2 9 1 3 4 6 5 8
1 3 8 5 9 6 2 4 7
6 5 4 7 2 8 3 9 1
5 4 6 3 1 2 7 8 9
3 9 1 8 6 7 5 2 4
2 8 7 4 5 9 1 6 3
```

PUZZLE 410

```
8 9 6 4 5 7 1 3 2
1 5 7 3 2 9 4 6 8
2 4 3 8 1 6 7 5 9
7 2 1 6 3 5 9 8 4
3 6 4 1 9 8 2 7 5
9 8 5 2 7 4 6 1 3
4 7 9 5 6 3 8 2 1
6 3 2 9 8 1 5 4 7
5 1 8 7 4 2 3 9 6
```

PUZZLE 411

```
4 6 8 1 9 5 3 7 2
9 5 7 6 2 3 8 1 4
1 2 3 7 8 4 5 6 9
2 1 9 3 4 8 6 5 7
8 4 5 2 6 7 9 3 1
7 3 6 9 5 1 4 2 8
6 8 2 5 7 9 1 4 3
5 9 1 4 3 2 7 8 6
3 7 4 8 1 6 2 9 5
```

PUZZLE 412

```
6 5 2 3 9 7 8 4 1
3 1 8 5 4 2 9 6 7
7 9 4 6 1 8 3 2 5
2 6 1 7 5 9 4 3 8
4 3 9 8 2 1 5 7 6
5 8 7 4 3 6 1 9 2
1 7 6 9 8 4 2 5 3
9 2 3 1 7 5 6 8 4
8 4 5 2 6 3 7 1 9
```

PUZZLE 413

```
1 5 3 2 7 4 8 6 9
4 9 7 6 8 3 1 5 2
2 8 6 9 1 5 7 4 3
5 7 9 3 4 1 6 2 8
6 3 1 8 9 2 5 7 4
8 2 4 7 5 6 9 3 1
9 6 8 4 2 7 3 1 5
3 4 5 1 6 8 2 9 7
7 1 2 5 3 9 4 8 6
```

PUZZLE 414

```
3 5 1 9 6 4 7 8 2
7 2 4 3 5 8 1 6 9
8 9 6 2 7 1 5 3 4
6 1 5 4 8 3 9 2 7
9 8 2 7 1 6 3 4 5
4 3 7 5 2 9 8 1 6
2 6 9 8 3 5 4 7 1
1 4 3 6 9 7 2 5 8
5 7 8 1 4 2 6 9 3
```

PUZZLE 415

```
1 6 2 4 8 3 7 9 5
4 9 7 5 2 1 8 6 3
5 8 3 6 9 7 4 1 2
6 4 5 7 3 9 1 2 8
2 3 1 8 5 4 6 7 9
9 7 8 1 6 2 5 3 4
3 1 6 9 4 5 2 8 7
7 5 9 2 1 8 3 4 6
8 2 4 3 7 6 9 5 1
```

PUZZLE 416

```
6 5 4 8 1 7 2 3 9
2 9 7 6 4 3 5 8 1
3 8 1 2 5 9 6 7 4
8 4 3 9 7 6 1 5 2
9 2 5 1 8 4 7 6 3
7 1 6 5 3 2 9 4 8
4 7 9 3 6 1 8 2 5
5 3 2 7 9 8 4 1 6
1 6 8 4 2 5 3 9 7
```

PUZZLE 417

```
8 6 2 9 4 7 1 3 5
5 9 3 2 6 1 4 8 7
7 4 1 3 5 8 2 6 9
1 7 9 8 2 5 3 4 6
2 8 6 4 7 3 9 5 1
3 5 4 1 9 6 7 2 8
9 3 7 5 8 2 6 1 4
6 1 8 7 3 4 5 . 2
4 2 5 6 1 9 8 7 3
```

PUZZLE 418

```
8 3 9 2 7 1 6 5 4
2 4 6 3 8 5 1 9 7
7 1 5 9 4 6 3 8 2
6 2 7 1 5 9 8 4 3
9 8 4 6 3 7 2 1 5
1 5 3 4 2 8 9 7 6
3 7 2 8 1 4 5 6 9
5 9 8 7 6 2 4 3 1
4 6 1 5 9 3 7 2 8
```

PUZZLE 419

```
6 7 1 2 3 4 5 9 8
5 2 9 7 8 6 3 1 4
4 3 8 5 1 9 7 6 2
1 6 5 8 9 2 4 3 7
2 9 4 3 5 7 1 8 6
3 8 7 6 4 1 2 5 9
8 4 2 1 6 3 9 7 5
9 1 6 4 7 5 8 2 3
7 5 3 9 2 8 6 4 1
```

PUZZLE 420

```
5 8 1 7 9 3 2 4 6
4 7 2 1 6 8 9 3 5
3 6 9 2 4 5 1 7 8
2 5 3 9 8 4 6 1 7
8 1 6 3 7 2 5 9 4
9 4 7 5 1 6 3 8 2
1 2 4 6 3 7 8 5 9
7 3 5 8 2 9 4 6 1
6 9 8 4 5 1 7 2 3
```

PUZZLE 421

5	8	3	2	6	4	1	7	9
1	2	7	5	3	9	4	6	8
9	4	6	7	1	8	3	2	5
7	1	5	9	8	6	2	3	4
2	3	9	1	4	5	6	8	7
8	6	4	3	7	2	9	5	1
3	9	8	4	2	7	5	1	6
6	5	1	8	9	3	7	4	2
4	7	2	6	5	1	8	9	3

PUZZLE 422

7	3	1	4	2	5	6	9	8
2	4	9	8	7	6	5	3	1
6	5	8	9	1	3	4	2	7
5	1	4	3	9	8	7	6	2
8	2	6	7	4	1	3	5	9
9	7	3	5	6	2	1	8	4
4	8	2	6	3	7	9	1	5
1	6	7	2	5	9	8	4	3
3	9	5	1	8	4	2	7	6

PUZZLE 423

7	1	2	3	4	5	8	9	6
9	3	6	2	8	7	4	5	1
5	4	8	6	9	1	2	7	3
1	7	3	9	5	2	6	8	4
8	6	5	1	3	4	7	2	9
4	2	9	7	6	8	1	3	5
6	9	4	8	7	3	5	1	2
3	8	1	5	2	6	9	4	7
2	5	7	4	1	9	3	6	8

PUZZLE 424

1	8	9	3	6	2	4	5	7
6	5	3	9	4	7	1	8	2
7	4	2	5	8	1	3	6	9
3	2	7	6	5	8	9	4	1
4	9	8	1	7	3	5	2	6
5	1	6	2	9	4	8	7	3
8	3	1	7	2	5	6	9	4
2	6	4	8	1	9	7	3	5
9	7	5	4	3	6	2	1	8

PUZZLE 425

3	6	2	1	8	9	7	4	5
4	9	1	2	5	7	8	6	3
7	8	5	6	4	3	2	9	1
9	4	7	8	3	1	5	2	6
1	5	8	4	6	2	3	7	9
6	2	3	7	9	5	4	1	8
8	1	9	5	2	4	6	3	7
2	3	6	9	7	8	1	5	4
5	7	4	3	1	6	9	8	2

PUZZLE 426

9	1	2	6	7	3	5	4	8
3	6	8	4	1	5	9	2	7
7	4	5	2	9	8	1	3	6
5	9	7	3	8	2	6	1	4
2	3	6	5	4	1	8	7	9
4	8	1	9	6	7	2	5	3
6	5	3	7	2	9	4	8	1
1	2	4	8	3	6	7	9	5
8	7	9	1	5	4	3	6	2

PUZZLE 427

5	1	7	3	8	4	2	9	6
2	6	8	9	5	7	4	1	3
4	9	3	6	1	2	8	5	7
3	4	1	5	9	6	7	8	2
9	8	2	7	4	1	3	6	5
7	5	6	2	3	8	1	4	9
6	3	4	1	2	9	5	7	8
1	7	5	8	6	3	9	2	4
8	2	9	4	7	5	6	3	1

PUZZLE 428

1	7	6	4	9	5	3	2	8
4	3	5	8	7	2	9	1	6
8	2	9	6	1	3	7	4	5
7	5	1	2	8	9	4	6	3
3	9	4	5	6	1	2	8	7
2	6	8	3	4	7	1	5	9
6	1	3	9	2	8	5	7	4
9	4	7	1	5	6	8	3	2
5	8	2	7	3	4	6	9	1

PUZZLE 429

9	2	1	4	8	7	3	6	5
7	4	3	1	6	5	9	8	2
5	8	6	9	2	3	7	4	1
8	5	4	3	1	2	6	9	7
3	1	7	8	9	6	5	2	4
6	9	2	7	5	4	1	3	8
1	6	5	2	4	9	8	7	3
2	3	8	6	7	1	4	5	9
4	7	9	5	3	8	2	1	6

PUZZLE 430

4	8	2	7	9	6	5	1	3
7	6	5	3	8	1	4	2	9
1	9	3	4	2	5	6	8	7
8	2	7	9	4	3	1	6	5
5	3	4	1	6	8	9	7	2
6	1	9	5	7	2	3	4	8
3	5	6	2	1	7	8	9	4
9	7	1	8	5	4	2	3	6
2	4	8	6	3	9	7	5	1

PUZZLE 431

6	3	1	7	8	4	5	9	2
5	4	9	3	2	1	6	7	8
2	7	8	6	9	5	4	1	3
8	9	7	2	4	3	1	6	5
3	5	4	9	1	6	8	2	7
1	6	2	5	7	8	3	4	9
4	2	3	1	5	9	7	8	6
9	1	5	8	6	7	2	3	4
7	8	6	4	3	2	9	5	1

PUZZLE 432

4	7	5	3	1	9	2	6	8
6	1	2	7	5	8	3	4	9
9	3	8	6	4	2	1	7	5
5	9	1	2	8	7	6	3	4
3	8	7	4	6	5	9	2	1
2	4	6	9	3	1	5	8	7
8	5	3	1	2	4	7	9	6
1	2	9	8	7	6	4	5	3
7	6	4	5	9	3	8	1	2

PUZZLE 433

1	5	2	8	6	7	4	3	9
6	7	9	4	3	2	5	8	1
8	3	4	9	1	5	6	7	2
3	2	5	6	9	1	8	4	7
9	6	1	7	4	8	3	2	5
4	8	7	2	5	3	9	1	6
7	9	3	1	8	6	2	5	4
2	4	8	5	7	9	1	6	3
5	1	6	3	2	4	7	9	8

PUZZLE 434

6	9	7	3	5	1	8	2	4
2	3	1	4	8	7	5	9	6
4	8	5	9	2	6	1	3	7
5	2	4	6	3	8	9	7	1
7	6	9	2	1	4	3	5	8
3	1	8	5	7	9	6	4	2
8	5	2	7	6	3	4	1	9
9	7	6	1	4	5	2	8	3
1	4	3	8	9	2	7	6	5

PUZZLE 435

5	2	4	7	6	1	9	3	8
3	9	8	2	5	4	6	7	1
1	7	6	9	3	8	5	4	2
2	8	9	4	1	6	3	5	7
6	4	3	5	2	7	1	8	9
7	1	5	8	9	3	4	2	6
8	3	1	6	4	2	7	9	5
9	6	2	3	7	5	8	1	4
4	5	7	1	8	9	2	6	3

PUZZLE 436

7	3	5	2	8	4	1	6	9
8	1	6	3	9	7	5	4	2
2	9	4	1	6	5	3	7	8
9	2	7	5	3	8	4	1	6
3	4	1	6	7	2	8	9	5
6	5	8	9	4	1	2	3	7
1	6	9	8	2	3	7	5	4
4	8	3	7	5	6	9	2	1
5	7	2	4	1	9	6	8	3

PUZZLE 437

6	3	5	1	4	7	2	8	9
7	8	2	9	5	3	6	4	1
9	4	1	6	2	8	7	5	3
1	5	8	7	6	2	9	3	4
3	6	7	5	9	4	1	2	8
2	9	4	8	3	1	5	7	6
4	1	3	2	7	6	8	9	5
5	7	6	4	8	9	3	1	2
8	2	9	3	1	5	4	6	7

PUZZLE 438

4	5	3	6	7	9	2	1	8
8	6	2	1	3	4	9	7	5
7	9	1	8	2	5	3	6	4
5	3	4	7	1	2	6	8	9
2	1	8	4	9	6	5	3	7
9	7	6	5	8	3	4	2	1
3	8	9	2	4	7	1	5	6
6	4	7	3	5	1	8	9	2
1	2	5	9	6	8	7	4	3

PUZZLE 439

4	1	8	5	9	3	6	7	2
2	6	9	1	7	4	3	5	8
3	7	5	2	8	6	1	4	9
5	8	7	6	1	9	2	3	4
1	4	3	7	5	2	9	8	6
6	9	2	4	3	8	5	1	7
8	2	4	3	6	5	7	9	1
9	5	1	8	2	7	4	6	3
7	3	6	9	4	1	8	2	5

PUZZLE 440

7	2	4	1	5	6	8	9	3
6	9	3	2	7	8	4	5	1
1	5	8	3	9	4	7	2	6
3	6	9	4	8	2	5	1	7
2	7	1	5	3	9	6	8	4
4	8	5	7	6	1	2	3	9
8	1	7	6	2	3	9	4	5
9	3	6	8	4	5	1	7	2
5	4	2	9	1	7	3	6	8

PUZZLE 441

9	2	3	1	8	4	6	5	7
1	6	5	7	2	9	8	3	4
7	8	4	3	5	6	2	9	1
2	4	6	5	9	7	1	8	3
8	1	7	4	3	2	9	6	5
3	5	9	6	1	8	7	4	2
6	9	1	2	4	5	3	7	8
5	7	2	8	6	3	4	1	9
4	3	8	9	7	1	5	2	6

PUZZLE 442

8	3	1	7	6	2	4	5	9
6	9	2	5	1	4	8	3	7
4	5	7	8	9	3	6	2	1
9	4	6	2	8	7	3	1	5
2	8	5	6	3	1	7	9	4
1	7	3	4	5	9	2	6	8
7	1	9	3	4	6	5	8	2
3	2	8	9	7	5	1	4	6
5	6	4	1	2	8	9	7	3

PUZZLE 443

2	5	6	1	3	7	8	9	4
1	7	4	8	9	6	2	5	3
9	3	8	4	2	5	6	1	7
5	1	9	7	6	8	3	4	2
4	8	2	3	1	9	5	7	6
7	6	3	5	4	2	1	8	9
8	2	7	6	5	4	9	3	1
6	4	1	9	8	3	7	2	5
3	9	5	2	7	1	4	6	8

PUZZLE 444

7	4	2	8	3	9	6	1	5
5	6	9	1	7	2	3	4	8
3	1	8	5	4	6	7	9	2
6	5	1	7	9	8	4	2	3
9	7	4	3	2	5	8	6	1
8	2	3	4	6	1	9	5	7
2	8	6	9	5	3	1	7	4
1	9	7	2	8	4	5	3	6
4	3	5	6	1	7	2	8	9

PUZZLE 445

9	3	2	8	5	6	1	4	7
8	1	5	4	3	7	9	2	6
6	7	4	2	9	1	5	8	3
3	5	8	6	2	9	4	7	1
4	2	7	1	8	5	3	6	9
1	9	6	3	7	4	8	5	2
5	8	9	7	1	2	6	3	4
2	6	1	5	4	3	7	9	8
7	4	3	9	6	8	2	1	5

PUZZLE 446

1	5	8	6	7	2	4	9	3
3	4	7	1	9	8	6	2	5
9	2	6	4	3	5	1	8	7
5	1	3	2	4	9	8	7	6
4	7	9	8	5	6	3	1	2
6	8	2	3	1	7	5	4	9
7	3	5	9	8	4	2	6	1
8	6	1	7	2	3	9	5	4
2	9	4	5	6	1	7	3	8

PUZZLE 447

1	9	8	6	2	4	7	5	3
7	3	2	1	5	9	6	8	4
5	6	4	8	7	3	2	9	1
2	8	3	7	9	6	1	4	5
4	5	6	2	1	8	9	3	7
9	1	7	4	3	5	8	6	2
3	4	1	9	8	2	5	7	6
8	7	5	3	6	1	4	2	9
6	2	9	5	4	7	3	1	8

PUZZLE 448

5	2	8	4	9	7	6	3	1
9	4	1	2	3	6	7	8	5
7	3	6	8	1	5	9	4	2
6	9	2	1	4	8	3	5	7
1	8	7	9	5	3	4	2	6
3	5	4	6	7	2	8	1	9
2	1	3	7	6	4	5	9	8
8	7	5	3	2	9	1	6	4
4	6	9	5	8	1	2	7	3

PUZZLE 449

8	2	1	3	5	9	6	7	4
9	7	3	6	4	8	2	1	5
5	6	4	7	1	2	9	8	3
4	5	7	8	2	6	1	3	9
2	9	8	1	3	4	7	5	6
3	1	6	9	7	5	8	4	2
1	4	5	2	9	7	3	6	8
7	8	9	5	6	3	4	2	1
6	3	2	4	8	1	5	9	7

PUZZLE 450

9	5	4	1	8	7	6	3	2
2	3	1	9	6	5	4	8	7
8	6	7	4	2	3	1	9	5
3	7	5	6	1	8	9	2	4
1	2	8	5	4	9	3	7	6
4	9	6	3	7	2	8	5	1
6	8	3	2	5	4	7	1	9
7	4	2	8	9	1	5	6	3
5	1	9	7	3	6	2	4	8

PUZZLE 451

3	8	5	4	2	7	9	6	1
1	2	9	3	8	6	5	7	4
7	4	6	9	5	1	8	2	3
8	6	3	1	7	5	2	4	9
2	9	7	6	3	4	1	5	8
4	5	1	8	9	2	6	3	7
5	1	8	2	4	3	7	9	6
6	7	4	5	1	9	3	8	2
9	3	2	7	6	8	4	1	5

PUZZLE 452

4	2	6	3	5	9	7	8	1
1	9	5	8	2	7	3	4	6
7	8	3	1	6	4	2	9	5
6	5	7	9	3	2	8	1	4
3	1	2	6	4	8	9	5	7
9	4	8	5	7	1	6	3	2
8	7	4	2	9	5	1	6	3
5	6	1	7	8	3	4	2	9
2	3	9	4	1	6	5	7	8

PUZZLE 453

6	5	3	7	1	2	9	8	4
7	4	8	5	9	3	2	6	1
2	9	1	6	4	8	3	7	5
8	1	5	9	2	4	6	3	7
9	7	6	3	8	5	1	4	2
4	3	2	1	7	6	8	5	9
5	6	7	2	3	1	4	9	8
3	2	4	8	5	9	7	1	6
1	8	9	4	6	7	5	2	3

PUZZLE 454

9	3	8	1	4	5	6	7	2
2	4	5	7	6	3	8	9	1
1	6	7	9	8	2	5	3	4
3	7	4	5	1	6	9	2	8
6	8	9	3	2	4	1	5	7
5	1	2	8	7	9	3	4	6
4	9	6	2	5	1	7	8	3
7	5	1	4	3	8	2	6	9
8	2	3	6	9	7	4	1	5

PUZZLE 455

1	2	6	4	8	7	9	3	5
8	3	7	5	9	1	2	6	4
5	9	4	2	3	6	8	7	1
4	8	9	6	7	5	3	1	2
7	6	5	3	1	2	4	9	8
3	1	2	8	4	9	6	5	7
9	4	3	7	5	8	1	2	6
2	5	1	9	6	4	7	8	3
6	7	8	1	2	3	5	4	9

PUZZLE 456

6	9	2	1	3	5	7	4	8
7	4	1	8	9	6	3	2	5
5	8	3	4	7	2	6	1	9
1	5	9	7	6	3	4	8	2
2	7	8	5	1	4	9	6	3
3	6	4	9	2	8	5	7	1
4	3	7	2	5	1	8	9	6
9	1	6	3	8	7	2	5	4
8	2	5	6	4	9	1	3	7

PUZZLE 457

8	7	1	3	5	2	4	9	6
9	2	5	7	6	4	1	8	3
3	4	6	9	1	8	5	7	2
7	8	9	1	3	5	2	6	4
6	5	4	2	9	7	8	3	1
1	3	2	4	8	6	7	5	9
5	9	3	8	4	1	6	2	7
2	1	8	6	7	3	9	4	5
4	6	7	5	2	9	3	1	8

PUZZLE 458

5	7	4	9	1	8	6	2	3
3	8	2	6	5	4	1	7	9
6	1	9	3	7	2	8	4	5
2	5	8	4	6	9	7	3	1
4	3	7	1	2	5	9	6	8
9	6	1	8	3	7	2	5	4
1	2	5	7	8	3	4	9	6
8	4	3	2	9	6	5	1	7
7	9	6	5	4	1	3	8	2

PUZZLE 459

6	3	7	5	1	8	2	9	4
4	1	8	2	3	9	6	5	7
9	2	5	4	6	7	3	1	8
3	5	9	6	7	1	8	4	2
1	7	2	8	9	4	5	3	6
8	4	6	3	5	2	1	7	9
7	6	3	9	8	5	4	2	1
5	9	4	1	2	6	7	8	3
2	8	1	7	4	3	9	6	5

PUZZLE 460

5	4	3	2	7	9	6	8	1
2	1	9	8	5	6	7	4	3
6	7	8	4	3	1	9	2	5
7	8	6	3	2	5	1	9	4
1	9	2	6	4	8	3	5	7
3	5	4	1	9	7	8	6	2
8	6	7	5	1	4	2	3	9
4	3	1	9	6	2	5	7	8
9	2	5	7	8	3	4	1	6

PUZZLE 461

9	4	6	1	2	3	7	8	5
2	3	1	7	8	5	9	6	4
5	8	7	6	4	9	1	2	3
3	9	2	5	6	8	4	1	7
8	6	5	4	1	7	3	9	2
1	7	4	3	9	2	8	5	6
6	5	3	8	7	1	2	4	9
7	1	9	2	5	4	6	3	8
4	2	8	9	3	6	5	7	1

PUZZLE 462

3	8	4	1	2	6	9	7	5
2	9	6	3	5	7	1	4	8
5	1	7	9	8	4	2	6	3
7	5	1	2	3	8	4	9	6
4	3	9	7	6	1	5	8	2
8	6	2	4	9	5	7	3	1
1	4	3	8	7	2	6	5	9
9	7	5	6	1	3	8	2	4
6	2	8	5	4	9	3	1	7

PUZZLE 463

5	1	8	6	3	7	2	4	9
4	7	9	5	1	2	8	6	3
6	2	3	9	8	4	5	7	1
7	5	1	4	9	8	3	2	6
3	6	4	1	2	5	7	9	8
9	8	2	3	7	6	1	5	4
2	3	7	8	6	9	4	1	5
8	9	5	7	4	1	6	3	2
1	4	6	2	5	3	9	8	7

PUZZLE 464

4	7	8	1	6	5	3	2	9
6	9	3	2	8	7	1	5	4
1	5	2	4	9	3	6	7	8
5	6	7	3	4	9	8	1	2
8	3	4	7	2	1	9	6	5
9	2	1	8	5	6	4	3	7
3	4	9	5	1	2	7	8	6
2	1	6	9	7	8	5	4	3
7	8	5	6	3	4	2	9	1

PUZZLE 465

3	5	6	2	7	1	9	4	8
2	9	7	4	3	8	5	1	6
1	4	8	9	5	6	7	2	3
5	1	9	6	2	3	4	8	7
6	7	4	5	8	9	2	3	1
8	2	3	1	4	7	6	5	9
7	6	2	3	1	5	8	9	4
4	8	1	7	9	2	3	6	5
9	3	5	8	6	4	1	7	2

PUZZLE 466

6	4	8	1	7	3	9	2	5
2	1	5	8	9	6	7	4	3
9	3	7	5	4	2	8	1	6
8	6	2	7	3	9	4	5	1
7	5	1	4	6	8	2	3	9
4	9	3	2	1	5	6	7	8
5	7	4	6	8	1	3	9	2
1	8	9	3	2	4	5	6	7
3	2	6	9	5	7	1	8	4

PUZZLE 467

2	4	5	1	8	9	6	3	7
6	3	8	7	2	5	9	1	4
9	7	1	6	4	3	8	2	5
3	6	9	8	5	1	4	7	2
8	5	2	3	7	4	1	9	6
4	1	7	9	6	2	3	5	8
1	8	6	2	9	7	5	4	3
5	2	3	4	1	6	7	8	9
7	9	4	5	3	8	2	6	1

PUZZLE 468

7	1	9	5	6	3	8	2	4
4	6	8	1	7	2	5	9	3
3	2	5	9	8	4	7	6	1
9	7	2	8	3	5	1	4	6
1	8	6	4	9	7	2	3	5
5	4	3	2	1	6	9	8	7
2	5	1	3	4	8	6	7	9
8	3	7	6	5	9	4	1	2
6	9	4	7	2	1	3	5	8

PUZZLE 469

2	7	1	8	4	6	3	9	5
8	5	4	3	1	9	6	2	7
9	6	3	2	7	5	1	4	8
7	4	9	5	2	3	8	6	1
5	1	2	6	8	4	9	7	3
6	3	8	1	9	7	4	5	2
1	9	6	7	5	8	2	3	4
3	8	5	4	6	2	7	1	9
4	2	7	9	3	1	5	8	6

PUZZLE 470

4	5	1	8	3	6	9	2	7
8	7	9	4	2	1	3	6	5
2	3	6	5	9	7	1	4	8
7	8	2	3	4	9	5	1	6
6	1	5	7	8	2	4	3	9
9	4	3	1	6	5	8	7	2
3	9	7	2	5	4	6	8	1
5	2	4	6	1	8	7	9	3
1	6	8	9	7	3	2	5	4

PUZZLE 471

5	8	1	7	3	4	6	2	9
3	2	6	5	1	9	7	4	8
7	4	9	2	6	8	1	3	5
4	6	3	1	8	7	9	5	2
1	9	8	6	5	2	4	7	3
2	5	7	4	9	3	8	6	1
9	7	5	8	2	6	3	1	4
6	3	2	9	4	1	5	8	7
8	1	4	3	7	5	2	9	6

PUZZLE 472

8	9	6	3	4	7	1	2	5
5	7	4	2	9	1	3	8	6
1	2	3	5	8	6	9	4	7
7	1	9	6	2	5	4	3	8
2	4	5	7	3	8	6	9	1
6	3	8	4	1	9	7	5	2
4	8	1	9	7	2	5	6	3
3	5	2	1	6	4	8	7	9
9	6	7	8	5	3	2	1	4

PUZZLE 473

8	6	2	5	7	4	3	1	9
3	7	5	9	2	1	4	6	8
4	1	9	6	8	3	2	5	7
9	2	4	7	3	6	5	8	1
5	3	7	2	1	8	6	9	4
1	8	6	4	9	5	7	2	3
7	4	8	1	5	2	9	3	6
6	5	1	3	4	9	8	7	2
2	9	3	8	6	7	1	4	5

PUZZLE 474

7	1	8	9	4	5	2	6	3
3	9	4	8	6	2	5	1	7
6	5	2	1	7	3	8	4	9
8	3	1	5	2	9	4	7	6
2	7	5	6	3	4	1	9	8
9	4	6	7	8	1	3	5	2
1	2	3	4	9	7	6	8	5
5	8	7	3	1	6	9	2	4
4	6	9	2	5	8	7	3	1

PUZZLE 475

5	7	1	8	2	6	3	9	4
6	8	4	9	1	3	7	5	2
9	2	3	7	4	5	1	8	6
3	4	2	1	6	8	9	7	5
7	6	5	3	9	2	8	4	1
1	9	8	4	5	7	2	6	3
4	3	6	2	7	9	5	1	8
8	1	7	5	3	4	6	2	9
2	5	9	6	8	1	4	3	7

PUZZLE 476

9	8	4	3	2	7	5	1	6
1	2	7	6	5	8	9	4	3
3	5	6	1	9	4	7	2	8
8	7	9	5	4	1	6	3	2
6	3	1	2	7	9	8	5	4
2	4	5	8	6	3	1	7	9
4	6	8	7	3	5	2	9	1
5	9	2	4	1	6	3	8	7
7	1	3	9	8	2	4	6	5

PUZZLE 477

8	6	4	3	1	9	7	5	2
7	2	1	6	5	8	4	3	9
9	3	5	4	2	7	1	6	8
6	4	9	7	8	5	3	2	1
1	7	8	2	6	3	9	4	5
2	5	3	9	4	1	8	7	6
4	1	7	5	9	6	2	8	3
3	9	6	8	7	2	5	1	4
5	8	2	1	3	4	6	9	7

PUZZLE 478

7	6	1	3	8	9	4	2	5
5	4	9	2	6	7	1	3	8
3	2	8	5	1	4	6	7	9
9	1	7	8	5	2	3	4	6
8	3	2	7	4	6	5	9	1
6	5	4	9	3	1	7	8	2
2	9	6	1	7	3	8	5	4
4	7	5	6	9	8	2	1	3
1	8	3	4	2	5	9	6	7

PUZZLE 479

6	2	8	9	5	4	1	3	7
7	3	1	6	2	8	9	4	5
5	9	4	7	1	3	2	8	6
9	8	7	1	6	2	4	5	3
2	4	3	8	9	5	6	7	1
1	5	6	4	3	7	8	2	9
4	6	2	5	7	9	3	1	8
8	7	9	3	4	1	5	6	2
3	1	5	2	8	6	7	9	4

PUZZLE 480

8	5	2	9	7	6	4	3	1
9	4	3	1	8	2	7	5	6
6	1	7	4	5	3	9	2	8
4	2	6	5	9	8	3	1	7
3	9	8	7	6	1	5	4	2
5	7	1	3	2	4	6	8	9
1	6	5	2	4	9	8	7	3
2	8	4	6	3	7	1	9	5
7	3	9	8	1	5	2	6	4

PUZZLE 481

2	3	6	7	8	9	5	4	1
8	5	7	2	4	1	3	9	6
1	4	9	5	3	6	8	2	7
4	9	5	3	6	8	7	1	2
7	1	3	4	9	2	6	5	8
6	2	8	1	5	7	4	3	9
9	7	4	8	2	5	1	6	3
3	6	1	9	7	4	2	8	5
5	8	2	6	1	3	9	7	4

PUZZLE 482

6	1	4	3	9	8	2	5	7
5	3	2	7	1	6	4	8	9
7	8	9	5	4	2	1	6	3
3	4	6	8	2	9	5	7	1
2	5	7	1	6	3	8	9	4
8	9	1	4	5	7	6	3	2
4	6	5	9	7	1	3	2	8
1	7	3	2	8	5	9	4	6
9	2	8	6	3	4	7	1	5

PUZZLE 483

7	3	5	1	6	2	8	9	4
1	9	4	5	8	7	2	6	3
2	6	8	4	3	9	5	1	7
9	4	2	3	5	6	7	8	1
3	5	1	9	7	8	4	2	6
6	8	7	2	4	1	3	5	9
8	7	3	6	1	5	9	4	2
4	2	6	8	9	3	1	7	5
5	1	9	7	2	4	6	3	8

PUZZLE 484

2	3	5	8	1	6	9	4	7
1	7	4	3	9	2	8	5	6
9	6	8	7	4	5	3	2	1
6	1	7	2	8	9	4	3	5
4	9	3	5	7	1	2	6	8
8	5	2	4	6	3	7	1	9
3	8	9	6	5	4	1	7	2
7	4	6	1	2	8	5	9	3
5	2	1	9	3	7	6	8	4

PUZZLE 485

9	3	1	2	7	5	6	4	8
6	4	5	9	8	3	2	1	7
7	8	2	6	1	4	3	5	9
8	1	9	4	2	6	5	7	3
2	5	7	8	3	1	4	9	6
3	6	4	5	9	7	8	2	1
1	7	6	3	5	2	9	8	4
4	2	8	1	6	9	7	3	5
5	9	3	7	4	8	1	6	2

PUZZLE 486

4	8	3	5	1	9	7	6	2
5	6	7	2	8	3	9	4	1
1	2	9	7	4	6	8	5	3
6	3	1	4	7	8	5	2	9
2	5	8	9	3	1	4	7	6
9	7	4	6	2	5	1	3	8
8	4	5	3	9	2	6	1	7
3	9	6	1	5	7	2	8	4
7	1	2	8	6	4	3	9	5

PUZZLE 487

6	8	5	4	2	3	9	1	7
1	3	2	9	8	7	4	6	5
4	9	7	6	5	1	3	2	8
7	5	9	1	4	8	2	3	6
3	1	4	2	7	6	8	5	9
8	2	6	3	9	5	1	7	4
5	4	3	7	1	9	6	8	2
2	6	8	5	3	4	7	9	1
9	7	1	8	6	2	5	4	3

PUZZLE 488

7	9	8	3	6	5	1	4	2
5	1	6	9	4	2	8	7	3
3	4	2	1	7	8	9	6	5
6	2	3	8	1	4	7	5	9
1	7	9	5	3	6	2	8	4
8	5	4	2	9	7	3	1	6
2	8	7	6	5	9	4	3	1
9	6	1	4	8	3	5	2	7
4	3	5	7	2	1	6	9	8

PUZZLE 489

7	8	1	9	5	6	4	2	3
5	4	3	1	2	8	6	9	7
9	6	2	3	7	4	5	1	8
6	7	9	5	1	3	2	8	4
3	1	5	4	8	2	7	6	9
8	2	4	6	9	7	1	3	5
2	3	7	8	4	1	9	5	6
1	5	8	7	6	9	3	4	2
4	9	6	2	3	5	8	7	1

PUZZLE 490

3	4	9	1	7	8	5	6	2
6	1	8	9	2	5	3	7	4
5	2	7	4	3	6	1	9	8
4	9	3	2	5	7	6	8	1
1	8	2	6	9	3	4	5	7
7	5	6	8	4	1	2	3	9
2	3	4	7	6	9	8	1	5
8	7	5	3	1	2	9	4	6
9	6	1	5	8	4	7	2	3

PUZZLE 491

8	4	2	5	9	1	7	6	3
7	5	9	6	3	8	2	4	1
1	3	6	2	4	7	5	9	8
4	7	5	9	1	3	6	8	2
2	1	8	7	5	6	9	3	4
6	9	3	8	2	4	1	5	7
9	8	4	1	7	5	3	2	6
5	6	1	3	8	2	4	7	9
3	2	7	4	6	9	8	1	5

PUZZLE 492

9	1	4	8	5	3	7	6	2
8	6	7	2	9	1	5	4	3
5	3	2	6	4	7	9	1	8
2	5	6	3	8	4	1	7	9
3	4	9	1	7	5	8	2	6
1	7	8	9	6	2	4	3	5
6	2	5	4	1	9	3	8	7
7	8	1	5	3	6	2	9	4
4	9	3	7	2	8	6	5	1

5	9	3	6	4	1	7	8	2
2	6	8	9	7	3	1	5	4
1	4	7	5	2	8	9	6	3
3	2	1	7	6	9	8	4	5
7	8	4	2	1	5	6	3	9
9	5	6	8	3	4	2	1	7
4	3	2	1	8	7	5	9	6
8	7	5	3	9	6	4	2	1
6	1	9	4	5	2	3	7	8

PUZZLE 493

6	9	8	7	3	1	4	5	2
5	3	7	6	2	4	8	1	9
4	2	1	9	8	5	3	7	6
3	7	2	1	5	8	6	9	4
1	4	9	2	7	6	5	3	8
8	6	5	4	9	3	1	2	7
9	1	3	8	6	7	2	4	5
2	8	4	5	1	9	7	6	3
7	5	6	3	4	2	9	8	1

PUZZLE 494

3	1	8	7	9	6	2	5	4
5	6	9	8	2	4	7	1	3
7	4	2	5	3	1	8	9	6
4	5	1	2	6	3	9	8	7
9	8	3	4	5	7	1	6	2
2	7	6	1	8	9	4	3	5
6	3	7	9	1	2	5	4	8
1	2	5	3	4	8	6	7	9
8	9	4	6	7	5	3	2	1

PUZZLE 495

3	2	9	4	5	6	1	8	7
6	8	7	1	2	3	5	4	9
5	4	1	9	8	7	2	6	3
7	3	6	5	1	4	9	2	8
9	1	4	8	7	2	6	3	5
8	5	2	3	6	9	4	7	1
1	7	3	2	4	5	8	9	6
2	6	8	7	9	1	3	5	4
4	9	5	6	3	8	7	1	2

PUZZLE 496

9	5	2	7	6	1	3	4	8
7	3	1	8	9	4	6	2	5
4	8	6	2	3	5	1	9	7
8	6	9	4	2	3	5	7	1
3	1	7	9	5	6	2	8	4
5	2	4	1	7	8	9	3	6
1	9	8	6	4	2	7	5	3
6	7	3	5	8	9	4	1	2
2	4	5	3	1	7	8	6	9

PUZZLE 497

5	2	1	9	8	6	7	4	3
4	6	9	3	2	7	1	8	5
7	3	8	5	1	4	2	9	6
8	7	5	6	4	1	3	2	9
6	9	2	7	5	3	4	1	8
3	1	4	2	9	8	6	5	7
1	5	6	4	7	9	8	3	2
9	4	7	8	3	2	5	6	1
2	8	3	1	6	5	9	7	4

PUZZLE 498

5	6	4	3	7	1	2	9	8
7	9	1	2	6	8	5	4	3
3	2	8	9	5	4	7	6	1
4	3	6	5	8	9	1	2	7
9	1	7	4	3	2	6	8	5
8	5	2	6	1	7	4	3	9
1	4	3	8	2	5	9	7	6
2	8	5	7	9	6	3	1	4
6	7	9	1	4	3	8	5	2

PUZZLE 499

7	6	9	2	4	1	5	3	8
1	3	4	5	8	6	9	7	2
2	8	5	7	9	3	4	1	6
6	7	3	8	2	4	1	9	5
9	4	8	6	1	5	7	2	3
5	1	2	9	3	7	6	8	4
8	2	1	4	5	9	3	6	7
4	9	7	3	6	8	2	5	1
3	5	6	1	7	2	8	4	9

PUZZLE 500

2	7	5	1	4	6	9	3	8
6	1	3	5	8	9	2	4	7
4	8	9	3	7	2	6	1	5
1	4	6	8	2	7	5	9	3
3	9	2	4	6	5	8	7	1
7	5	8	9	1	3	4	6	2
8	3	4	2	9	1	7	5	6
9	6	1	7	5	8	3	2	4
5	2	7	6	3	4	1	8	9

PUZZLE 501

3	8	1	2	7	5	9	6	4
9	7	5	4	6	3	8	2	1
4	6	2	1	8	9	7	5	3
2	3	9	7	1	4	5	8	6
6	5	8	3	9	2	4	1	7
7	1	4	8	5	6	2	3	9
5	2	6	9	3	7	1	4	8
1	9	3	5	4	8	6	7	2
8	4	7	6	2	1	3	9	5

PUZZLE 502

4	8	5	7	1	3	6	2	9
6	7	2	9	4	8	1	5	3
1	3	9	2	5	6	7	4	8
2	9	8	5	3	7	4	6	1
7	5	4	1	6	9	8	3	2
3	6	1	8	2	4	9	7	5
8	4	6	3	9	5	2	1	7
9	1	3	4	7	2	5	8	6
5	2	7	6	8	1	3	9	4

PUZZLE 503

6	7	2	9	8	3	1	4	5
1	5	9	6	4	7	2	3	8
8	3	4	1	5	2	7	6	9
9	8	6	2	7	1	4	5	3
4	1	3	5	9	6	8	7	2
7	2	5	8	3	4	6	9	1
2	9	1	4	6	5	3	8	7
3	4	8	7	2	9	5	1	6
5	6	7	3	1	8	9	2	4

PUZZLE 504

7	1	2	3	5	4	8	6	9
3	5	8	7	9	6	1	4	2
4	9	6	1	2	8	5	3	7
1	2	9	6	3	7	4	5	8
8	3	5	4	1	2	9	7	6
6	7	4	9	8	5	3	2	1
2	4	1	5	6	9	7	8	3
5	6	3	8	7	1	2	9	4
9	8	7	2	4	3	6	1	5

PUZZLE 505

1	8	2	3	6	7	5	4	9
7	6	9	8	4	5	3	1	2
4	3	5	1	9	2	7	6	8
9	1	3	5	2	8	6	7	4
8	7	6	4	3	9	1	2	5
2	5	4	7	1	6	9	8	3
3	4	8	6	5	1	2	9	7
5	9	1	2	7	4	8	3	6
6	2	7	9	8	3	4	5	1

PUZZLE 506

8	5	9	7	6	1	4	2	3
6	4	3	2	8	5	9	7	1
2	7	1	4	9	3	5	8	6
3	8	6	1	4	7	2	9	5
5	9	7	3	2	8	1	6	4
4	1	2	6	5	9	8	3	7
9	3	8	5	7	4	6	1	2
1	6	4	9	3	2	7	5	8
7	2	5	8	1	6	3	4	9

PUZZLE 507

6	9	4	2	5	3	1	7	8
3	8	1	4	6	7	5	2	9
2	7	5	8	1	9	6	4	3
4	6	2	5	3	1	9	8	7
1	3	8	7	9	2	4	5	6
9	5	7	6	8	4	2	3	1
7	2	6	1	4	8	3	9	5
5	4	9	3	7	6	8	1	2
8	1	3	9	2	5	7	6	4

PUZZLE 508